AUTOMOBILE DRIVING
Self-Taught

DISCARD

Produced by the
Automotive Book Department
JOHN MILTON, *Managing Editor*

CHILTON BOOK COMPANY

Philadelphia   New York   London

Introduction

Now and then it falls to the lot of the observant editorial eye to find a jewel of automotive literature that has for years been wasting away on a dusty shelf, unheard of and unappreciated by modern automobile enthusiasts, and generally unobtainable. To bring to renewed life such a find for the benefit of the thousands today who care about such things, is clearly seen as a duty . . . a duty performed with pleasure.

From its title page to its ultimate chapter, this book is the same as the original edition of 1909. What the reader has in hand is what the reader-automobilist of 1909 pored over and looked to for instruction, and what he depended upon for his very life (amid a world of frightened horses) as well as for the life of his precious car. If at times to the modern reader the instructions for care and upkeep seem quaint or incredible, let it be said that our own jolly little world of mag wheels will seem equally at odds and amusing to later generations who will ride their individual light beams to wherever they wish to go.

In the meanwhile *Automobile Driving Self-Taught* is to be savored and enjoyed by all who have a sense of the fitness of things as they surround and concern that great institution of American life —the automobile.

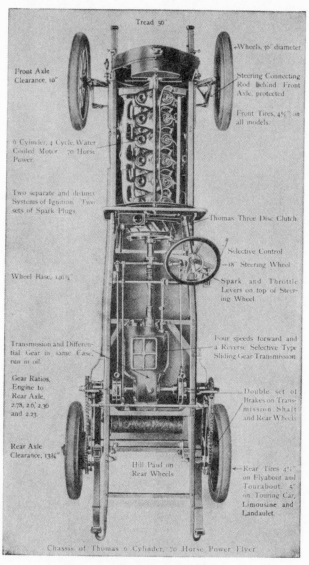

Tread 50"

Wheels, 36" diameter

Front Axle
Clearance, 10"

Steering Connecting
Rod behind Front
Axle, protected

Front Tires, 4½" on
all models.

6 Cylinder, 4 Cycle, Water
Cooled Motor. 70 Horse
Power.

Two separate and distinct
Systems of Ignition. Two
sets of Spark Plugs.

Thomas Three Disc Clutch

Selective Control
—18" Steering Wheel

Spark and Throttle
Levers on top of Steer-
ing Wheel.

Wheel Base, 140½"

Transmission and Differential Gear in same Case,
run in oil.

Four speeds forward and
a Reverse Selective Type
Sliding Gear Transmission

Gear Ratios,
Engine to
Rear Axle,
2.78, 2.6, 2.36
and 2.23.

Double set of
Brakes on Trans-
mission Shaft
and Rear Wheels

Rear Axle
Clearance, 13¾"

Hill Pawl on
Rear Wheels

Rear Tires 4½"
on Flyabout and
Tourabout. 5"
on Touring Car,
Limousine and
Landaulet.

Chassis of Thomas 6 Cylinder, 70 Horse Power Flyer.

A 1909 Model Chassis,

AUTOMOBILE DRIVING
SELF-TAUGHT

An Exhaustive Treatise on the Operation,
Management, and Care of
Motor Cars.

By

THOMAS H. RUSSELL, M. E., LL. B.

Former Editor of "Modern Machinery"; Editor of "The
American Cyclopedia of the Automobile"; Author
of "History of the Automobile," "Automobile
Motors and Mechanism," "Ignition,
Timing, and Valve Setting," "Motor
Boats: Construction and
Operation," etc.

1909

THE CHARLES C. THOMPSON CO. (Not Inc.)
CHICAGO, U. S. A.

Preface

As comfort and safety in automobiling depend to a very
large extent upon the skill of the driver, it should be the aim
of everyone who undertakes to drive a car to acquire a knowledge of the approved methods of driving.

The object of this book is to present such information in
a convenient, practical manner, so as to make it comparatively easy for any motorist to acquire skill in the management and care of his machine. Study and practice combined
will surely develop the expertness which is needed nowadays
at the wheel, being demanded alike by the interests of the
automobilist and of the non-motoring public. The careless or
ignorant driver is a menace, not only to the safety of the
public, but also to that of his passengers. The daily experience of every motorist demonstrates the need for carefulness
in driving and there is no longer any excuse for ignorance.

The methods of driving prescribed in this work are those
that have been found best in actual experience on the road.
From these pages the motorist can learn how to start, drive
and manage his car under all conceivable circumstances. The
best methods of caring for the car when not in use are also
plainly shown, as well as the manner in which a car should
be laid up when necessary.

Several chapters are devoted to the causes and remedies
for various difficulties that may be met with in starting the
engine, also those due to loss of power. Causes of involuntary
stops are likewise indicated and the proper remedies pre-

scribed. The properties and economical use of gasolene are discussed and many valuable hints and tips for the gasolene consumer are given. Then the operating mechanism of a modern car is described and the various forms of change speed gear are made clear by non-technical text and plain illustrations. There is also an interesting chapter on the choice of a car, intended for the benefit of those who contemplate entering the ever-growing ranks of the automobile fraternity.

Thus it will be seen that this work is not only a complete textbook for self-tuition in the art of automobile driving, but also a handy reference book in cases of trouble due to difficulty in starting, involuntary stops, loss of power, etc., and a storehouse of practical information on the care and maintenance of the motor car.   T. H. R.

Contents

PART I.

AUTOMOBILE DRIVING.

The best way to learn to drive a car is a question that must be decided by individual circumstances. It is generally agreed, however, though not regarded as essential, that the novice should begin with a small light car, if convenient, and acquire confidence in the use of such a machine before undertaking the management of the heavier, costlier and more complex cars. This does not necessarily imply that the man who has never driven an automobile must needs first buy a light car before indulging the desire of his heart to own a powerful, commodious touring machine. Facilities for learning to drive on a small car abound in our cities and towns nowadays, and automobile agents are usually ready to put prospective customers in the way of receiving preliminary instruction on light machines at expert hands. For his own comfort and safety's sake, as well as for considerations of public safety, no man should attempt to drive a car of any size until he has informed himself pretty fully on its details of construction and methods of control.

It should be clearly understood that some of the general instructions under this head of "Driving," as well as many of the hints and "tips" which follow, have been written to apply especially to cars of moderate power, such as novices are usually recommended to learn upon. It must be remembered also that thousands of cars made in earlier years of the automobile industry are still in daily use and are constantly changing ownership, so that the mechanism, driving and control of such cars properly receive due consideration in these pages.

At the same time the vast majority of the instructions apply to the driving of any car irrespective of size, though each individual make has its peculiarities which cannot be covered under a general heading.

"Drive slowly until fully competent" is a general instruction to beginners which is all-important and should never be neglected.

Nerve, judgment, experience, and consideration for the public are all necessary for good driving. The mere steering of the car on a dry road where there is no traffic is as simple as child's play, but it is when difficulties arise suddenly that the qualities above enumerated become necessary.

Before Starting.

Before starting a car for the day, first examine the gasolene, lubricating oil and water tanks, and grease cups to make sure they are fully charged. See that the engine and other vital parts are lubricated properly. Make a cursory examination of the wires, batteries, etc., to determine if all the connections are tight. Make sure, too, that the gear lever is in the neutral notch, and that the hand-brake is on hard. Make a general inspection of the car so far as time permits. Then turn on the gasolene, switch on the current, and retard the sparking so as to prevent the risk of back fire. It sometimes happens that the engine will not start freely with the ignition retarded to the fullest. In such a case the lever should be advanced very slightly until the best position has been found by experiment, bearing in mind always that the further it is advanced the greater will be the risk of a back fire.

The carburation lever, when such is fitted, is the next that requires attention. Seeing that the piston can only be made to travel at a comparatively slow rate when operated by the starting handle, it is necessary to put the carburation lever in such a position that nearly the entire volume of air passes round the spraying nipple. Most carbureters nowadays are automatic, so that the correct proportion of air and gas are approximately assured at every revolution. It may, however, be necessary to slightly alter the adjustment of the air supply.

The throttle lever should then be placed in the position which has been found by experiment to be the best one for starting purposes.

Starting the Engine.

The next operation is to start the engine. First operate the small plunger fitted over the float chamber of the carbureter for the purpose of insuring an adequate supply of gasolene vapor, which otherwise might not be sufficient, owing to the impossibility of operating the engine at a fast speed by hand, and the consequent feeble suction. It is best, however, not to "flood" the carbureter in the ordinary acceptance of the term, for if there is an over supply of gasolene the mixture may prove so rich that the engine will not start. It is only necessary to get the mixture rich enough to be easily ignited. Experience will show to what extent the carbureter need be "tickled" to insure the best starting results.

Next, with the handle at the lowest point, grasp it in the right hand with the fingers pointing in the direction in which the handle revolves, and, with the left hand, grip the adjacent dumb-iron so as to give a good purchase. Then standing well clear of the handle give a short, sharp pull upward, more in the nature of a jerk than an ordinary pull, and drop the handle the moment it gets to the highest point.

Should the engine not start after several trials "tickle" the carbureter again and try once more. If the engine still proves refractory, squirt a little kerosene or gasolene—the latter is the most efficacious— through the compression cocks. If this fails, examine the ignition system, especially the plugs. Note that the handle should always be pulled upward, never pushed downward, and it is advisable to place the thumb on the same side of the handle as to the fingers, in case of a back fire. Some motorists adopt the practice of winding the handle until the engine starts. It is a dangerous practice however, for, should a back fire occur, a sprained or broken wrist may result.

Most two, four and six cylinder, as well as some of the later types of one-cylinder cars are provided with a compression release arrangement to facilitate starting. This is actuated by a rod projecting through the frame under the bonnet in front of the car. It is held in position by a stop while the handle is being turned. When the motor starts, return the rod to its normal position.

Multi-cylinder engines, while still hot, can, as a rule, be started by switching on the current, and also when cold, but in this case the driver should give the starting handle a turn or two first, with the ignition switched off, so as to draw in a charge. In the case of one or two cylinder engines it is also advisable to draw in a charge before the ignition is switched on, and the operator should make sure that the piston is on the compression stroke before finally attempting to get the engine in motion.

Advancing the Spark.

Having started the engine the ignition should be very slightly advanced to prevent overheating At the same time the throttle lever should be operated until the engine is running as slowly as possible. The driver should then take his seat in the car, depress the clutch pedal, take the hand brake out of operation, move the gear lever into the low speed notch, open the throttle to a medium position, and let the clutch in as smoothly and gradually as possible. The practice of starting on any gear but the low one, except on a down grade, is not to be recommended, as it strains the engine and entire transmission system.

How to Change Speeds.

It is absolutely essential that the beginner should carefully cultivate the art of changing his gears correctly if he desires to become an expert driver and to drive economically. The sliding type of change speed gear which is now almost universal is, from a mechanical point of view, a somewhat brutal system, because, if the driver is not skilful and careful, he is bound to bring the edges of the gear wheels on the primary and secondary shaft into fierce contact while they are revolving at different speeds. This will cause great wear and may even chip off portions of the teeth. The act of changing properly is simply a knack, requiring some experience and a quick, delicate and sympathetic touch. The beginner should, if possible, learn this on a small car.

Before making his initial attempt he should endeavor to grasp the difficulties of the situation The problem is as follows: There are two trains of gear wheels (see Change Speed Gear) revolving at varying speeds according to the ratio between the two gear wheels which happen to be in mesh. The change is effected by taking these gear wheels out of mesh, and causing two other gear wheels to mesh whose ratios to each other are not the same as the previous pair, and which consequently are revolving at different speeds at the moment immediately preceding the change. To effect a clean change, therefore, it is essential that at the moment when the two gear wheels are moved into contact they are revolving at approximately their respective "in-mesh" speeds. Otherwise the faces of the teeth will grind against each other.

Different makes of cars generally vary slightly as regards the movements necessary for perfect changing, and consequently we shall describe the best methods for certain types of cars well known in the United States and Europe. This will prove sufficient guide as to general principles. Taking the Peugeot car as a typical example, we will describe the best methods for manipulating the gears. Having started the engine, its speed should be reduced to a minimum prior to declutching, so as to insure that the clutch shaft ceases to revolve. The gear lever should then be moved gently into the low speed notch. If there is any difficulty in getting the gear teeth to engage without grating, the clutch should be let into operation for a moment, and another attempt made, or failing that, the driver should get into the reverse and then immediately go right forward into the low speed. For the second speed the engine should be run at its normal speed, and the clutch taken out sharply and decisively. The change also should be made with decision, the vital point being that both movements should synchronize. At the same time the movement should not be violent.

On the third and fourth speeds, the change should also be decisive, the gear lever being pushed rapidly forward at the moment of declutching. Any hesitation will cause the car to lose impetus, and consequently the engine will not take up its load well, while in many cases the teeth will grind. As regards the top speed, it is direct in the case of the cars manufactured by the Peugeot firm, and is obtained by means of dog clutches. If the action of changing is decisive there is very little risk of missing this gear, but if the operator does miss, the only plan is to go right back on to the third speed, let the clutch in for a moment, and then make another attempt at changing. When changing from a low to a higher speed, it is not well to let the clutch in instantaneously, especially on an up-grade, as the strain will then be considerable, and the speed taken off the engine. There should be just a suspicion of slip to enable the drive to be taken up smoothly. The driver should not change too soon to a higher gear on an ascent. He should wait until he is sure that the engine will take the higher gear without laboring.

In changing down the method is somewhat different. The operator should be careful that the speed at which the car is traveling approximates to that to which he is about to descend, and consequently if he is changing on the level, for the sake of traffic or such like, he should slow down the car by means of the throttle or by taking the clutch out momentarily. In the latter case it facilitates changing to let the clutch into operation again for a fraction of a second before effecting the change. As regards the actual change, whether on the level or on an ascent, the method of declutching is different from that adopted when changing up. Instead of the clutch being taken out firmly, rapidly, and decisively, the foot action should be more in the nature of a tap, only just sufficient to relieve the pressure of the pinions on each other, so as to facilitate their coming out of mesh in response to the pressure of the gear lever, actuated at the same time. The change speed lever should not be operated quite so decisively, but at the same time without hesitation, the object aimed at being to bring the pinions into contact at the exact moment when the primary gear shaft has slowed to such an extent that the smaller pinion, which is about to be brought into mesh, is revolving approximately at the same rate as the larger pinion on the secondary gear shaft. In getting from the fourth to the third, and the third to the second, it is very unusual to miss changing, but in getting from the second to the first or lowest speed, the smallness of the pinion on the primary shaft, and the likelihood of the car traveling too fast for the low speed, make a change more difficult. The operator should, therefore, wait until the pace has dropped, and if the gears grate should give two or three rapid taps to the clutch pedal, at the same time applying gentle pressure to the change-speed lever, when the gear will easily go home. The engine should not be raced just before the change is made, neither should it be throttled down but should be run at about its normal speed. Should, however, the driver wish to pick up quickly on an ascent he will find it advantageous, just as the gears mesh, to race the engine, at the same time not slamming the clutch in, but letting it slip slightly for the first few yards.

In the light Rover, a typical British machine, the gears, which consist of three forward and a reverse, have to be operated in a somewhat different manner. In changing from the first to the second the action should be comparatively steady, and the clutch taken out sharply. In changing from the second to the high speed the action should be very rapid and sharp, both as regards the clutch and the gear lever. In changing down, the greatest difficulty is getting cleanly from the third to the second. It is essential that the speed of the car should have dropped sufficiently; in fact, a better change can be effected if the speed is allowed to drop below the pace of the second speed. The lever should be operated comparatively slowly, the driver feeling his way, and operating the clutch pedal with a series of little taps should the pinions not slip into mesh smoothly. No attempt should be made to force the gear should the pinions grind, but the driver should continue tapping the clutch pedal and pressing gently on the lever.

In fact, after a touch or two to the clutch pedal to allow the gear wheels in engagement to come out of mesh easily the change can often be effected while the clutch is actually in operation. This applies to some other cars also, more especially when a driver wants to change from a high speed to a lower one when running light on the level—in traffic, for example—or down hill.

In the case of the English Rover it is not difficult to get into the low speed, and the operation is somewhat the same as already described.

In the Argyll car, manufactured in Glasgow, Scotland, there are three speeds forward and a reverse, and it is an easy car to effect a clean change with, due to the special system adopted. In the case of the second and third speeds the gear wheels are always in mesh, and the change is effected by dog clutches. The low speed is, however, operated by sliding pinions. The most important feature of the design, from a gear changing point of view, is that the operating gear is spring controlled. The driver, therefore, cannot force either the gear-wheel faces or the dog-clutch faces into contact with each other. All he can do is to bring them into position, so to speak, and the spring pressure slips them into engagement when the right moment arrives.

In the type fitted to the lighter De Dion cars the pinions are always in mesh, and expanding clutches effect the change. In the Winton type, also, the wheels are in mesh, and the gear changing is effected by bringing friction cone clutches into operation, as described under Change Speed Gear. In both these types it is advisable to make the change gradually, so as to allow the clutch to slip slightly at first and thus take up the drive smoothly.

In the epicyclic type, as fitted to the English Lanchester and the early Duryea, Oldsmobile, and other American cars, the gear wheels are also in mesh, and the application of band brakes, which must be gradually applied, effects the change.

Generally speaking, changes "up" should be sharp and quick to prevent any loss of momentum in the car, while changes "down" should be effected more slowly, just allowing the gears, under slight hand pressure, to slip in of their own accord when the engine speed has increased to the necessary extent. There should then be no noise.

Use of the Clutch.

The condition of the clutch is all important. If it is fierce it is impossible to take up the drive gradually, and great strain is caused to the engine, gear, transmission system and tires. The care of the clutch is an essential factor of good driving and is fully dealt with elsewhere under this heading. In starting, the clutch should be brought into operation so gradually that the car moves off without the slightest jerk. In gear changing, the clutch action should be sympathetic and should synchronize with the gear-changing effort. There should be no undue hesitation in letting the clutch into operation again, but at the same time this should be effected so that there is no jerk in taking up the drive. In changing up, especially, this is important. If the change is very rapid when changing down, the clutch can as a rule be let right home, for the pace of the car will not have dropped below the speed represented by the gear on to which the driver has dropped. If, however, the driver is unskilful and changes slowly, or if the gears are badly designed or constructed and do not therefore change at once, it is essential that the clutch should be let slip slightly so as to take up the drive gradually, otherwise there will be an injurious jerk. On the other hand, if the clutch is slipped too much the car may continue to slow down—in extreme cases to such an extent that the engine will not be able to take the gear without laboring unduly—which may necessitate dropping on to a still lower gear. Also, if the clutch is withdrawn in traffic, so that the pace slows, it should be let in again very gradually. Or if the car is running free downhill, and has attained a greater pace than corresponds with the speed of the particular gear which happens to be in mesh, the same precaution should be observed.

Clutch slipping, of course, causes a certain amount of wear

on the clutch faces, and consequently should not be unduly resorted to, as when checking the pace in traffic or nursing the car over the crest of a hill in order to avoid the necessity of changing gear. Generally speaking, it is better to change under such circumstances. Properly constructed plate or disk clutches, working in oil, can be slipped to a greater extent without undue wear than cone or expanding clutches. In fact, in the case of some plate-clutches drivers report that they have found it possible by slipping the clutch to run at such a crawling pace on the high gear as would otherwise be impossible without causing the engine to labor, and nevertheless, after a whole season's use, the wear was hardly appreciable.

The Control Levers.

The power of the engine is affected by the control levers, and consequently excessive movement of the same, unless carrid out gradually, will vary the power of the engine so rapidly as to cause undue strain on engine, transmission system, and tires, just as in the case of a fierce clutch let into engagement suddenly. In the case of some carbureters such sudden and excessive movement will absolutely upset the carburation, and consequently may affect the power temporarily to such an extent that the driver who thus advances his ignition and carburation levers to the utmost, with the object of getting the maximum of power, may get an exactly opposite result—in extreme cases to such an extent that it may be necessary to change on to a lower speed to allow the engine to pick up again. Such conditions are sometimes accompanied by popping in the carbureter. Of course, some automatic carbureters are proof against such inconsiderate treatment, but there are very few which are not influenced more or less.

In some cases the governor is designed to control the ignition, carburation, and throttle, or any two of them in synchronism, with the object of making the control as nearly proof as possible against misuse.

Taking it for granted, however, that there are control levers for the driver to operate, we shall now give a few detailed hints as to their manipulation.

The ignition lever should never be fully retarded, except when starting the engine. The reason is simple. Under such circumstances the combustion of the gas takes place so late that much of the power is lost, and it is still in an ignited and partly consumed condition when the exhaust valve opens, with the result that the engine is excessively heated. On the other hand, the ignition should never be advanced to the full unless the engine is running at its highest speed. It will, therefore, be seen that a medium position is the best for general purposes, whether the throttle is fully opened or not, and should only be altered when the speed of the engine is approaching its maximum or minimum. When the engine is running idle, the lever might be midway between the medium and the fully retarded position, and when it is running faster, but not accelerated, it might be between the medium and the fully advanced position.

Briefly, the driver should bear in mind that to get the best results he should use the best possible mixture and explode it at the best possible time, that is, just as the piston is about to descend on its down stroke. He must also bear in mind that combustion is not instantaneous, and that the more the mixture errs from theoretically correct proportions the slower is the combustion, so that in such cases it may be necessary to advance the ignition somewhat further than if the mixture is perfect. The same result follows if the spark is very feeble through the battery running out, short circuits, or some such cause. He must also bear in mind, that in the case of high tension ignition—whether by coil and battery or by magneto —there is a distinct "lag" in the coil, which slightly delays the period of combustion, whereas with low tension magneto ignition there is no lag. There is one other point too in connection with the latter ignition. The spark is rather of the nature of flame than a spark, so that the combustion is more instantaneous. Therefore, the range of effective movement of the ignition lever is reduced. This peculiarity is so pronounced that some firms make no provision for varying the timing of the spark except for starting purposes. This subject is more easily mastered after a study of the various ignition systems.

The carburation lever, where such is fitted, controls the quality of the gas, and the operator should seek by experiment to insure the best possible mixture under all conditions, always bearing in mind that it is better to err on the side of too much air than too much gas, because an over-rich mixture not only prevents the engine from giving its full power, as in the case of an over-weak mixture, but has the additional disadvantage that it fouls the plugs, combustion chamber, etc., and causes overheating, in addition to a most pungent smell.

As a rule the throttle control is connected up to the governor, and a throttle lever on the steering wheel restrains the action of the governor, so that the driver can by its manipulation make the engine run at any speed between the minimum and the maximum. In other cars an accelerator lever or pedal is fitted, by means of which the driver can cut the governor out of action altogether, and the engine will then, practically speaking, race. In this case the throttle lever is used, through the medium of the governor, to vary the speed and consequently the power of the engine within the normal and minimum speeds, the ignition lever being operated in sympathy.

The accelerator lever or pedal should only be used to race the engine under exceptional circumstances, that is to say, when the very highest speed of the car is desired, or when the driver wishes to rush a hill. Many automobilists possessed by the speed craze habitually race their engines, thus causing excessive wear and tear. It is a great mistake, and results in infinite trouble later on.

As already mentioned, the throttle lever should be operated gradually, whether it is desired to increase or diminish the speed of the engine. Sometimes, but rarely, an entirely independent throttle lever is used to control the speed of the engine, and it also should be moved gradually.

Use of Engine Control Levers.

The speed and power of the engine are controlled by means of hand and foot levers, as follows:

Ignition—On steering wheel.

Throttle—On steering wheel.

Governor—For cutting out the governor at any desired point.

Carburation—Generally on dashboard; used for varying the mixture, but now seldom fitted owing to the popularity of automatic carbureters. As a rule, it is not connected with any other control. In the Talbot, however, the extra air inlet is inter-connected with the ignition lever, so that on advancing the spark, as when the engine is running fast, extra air is admitted.

The Accelerator Pedal may act as follows:

(1) On the throttle direct, so that, although the throttle lever on the steering wheel is set at a partially open position of the throttle, the depression of the accelerator pedal will open it fully without altering the position of the lever, and when the pedal is released the throttle will return to the position decided by the position of the lever on the wheel.

(2) On the ignition, so that normally the engine runs with the ignition partially retarded, but when the accelerator pedal is depressed the ignition is advanced. In this case the accelerator pedal is generally coupled up to the throttle as well as to the ignition, and there is no ignition lever on the steering wheel.

(3) On the governor (when such is fitted), which is set normally to keep the engine from running above a predetermined speed. In this case the accelerator pedal is aranged to hold the governor up against the action of centrifugal force, and on being put in action allows the engine to attain a higher speed than that to which the governor would otherwise have restrained it.

(4) In combination with a hand lever on the steering wheel, which will control the point at which the governor will not allow any further rise in the speed of the engine, and which

can also be used to control the engine speed should the driver elect not to use the accelerator pedal. At whatever point the lever is left the governor will cut out, but if the accelerator pedal is depressed, it nullifies this action and allows the engine to increase its speed up to the maximum at which it is set to run.

(5) Or it may be coupled both to throttle and ignition as before, so as to advance ignition and open the throttle more fully than they are set by the two hand levers on the steering wheel, and, when released, to return them to the positions fixed by the position of these levers. In this case there is no governor.

(6) It may also be used in connection with the governor which controls the throttle, as in case (3), and at the same time to advance the ignition.

(7) It may also be used in the same way to advance the ignition as well as to put the governor in operation as described in case (4), where a hand lever is used in combination with a governor.

Principles of Gear Changing.

It should be understood that whenever two wheels have to be put into gear with each other, their edges, or periphery, or teeth, whichever term may be used, should be moving at the same speed. This does not mean that the wheels should be rotating at the same speed. Only when both wheels are of the same diameter will this be the case. When they are of different sizes the smaller wheel will rotate faster than the other, though the speed of its teeth—that is, the distance they travel—will necessarily be the same during any given period of time. Any tooth on the small wheel will, of course, travel a complete circle, while a tooth on the bigger wheel will not have completed a circle on account of the larger circumference.

The Peripheral Speed of two unequal wheels in gear with each other remains the same.

The Angular Velocity, or the time taken by the wheel to travel through a certain angle of its circle, varies.

The beginner should first get the following facts into his head:

WHEN CHANGING UP—Neutral to low speed. Primary shaft revolving; secondary shaft idle. Low speed to second; second to third; third to fourth. Primary shaft with its gear wheels running comparatively fast; secondary shaft comparatively slowly. As one goes up the scale the difference in speed of the shafts becomes less.

WHEN CHANGING DOWN—Primary shaft with its gear wheels running comparatively slowly; secondary shaft with its gear wheels comparatively fast. As one descends the scale the difference in speed of the shafts increases. In most cases, when running on the fourth speed, the primary and secondary shafts are revolving at the same rate. The effect is the same, however, as the primary shaft has to be slowed to allow the smaller third speed wheel on it to mesh with the larger third speed wheel on the secondary.

To make a clean change, therefore, when changing up, depress the clutch firmly and rapidly, and operate the lever with deliberation at first, but quicker when changing from second to third and third to fourth.

When changing down, take the clutch out comparatively slowly, so as to allow it to slip, and operate the lever gently and deliberately.

A study of the appended diagrams, Figs. 1, 2, 3, 4, and 5, will make our meaning plainer. A, B, C, and D represent the gear wheels on the primary shaft of a four-speed Panhard type of gear, in which the drive is indirect on all speeds; A1, B1, C1, and D1 represent the gear wheels on the secondary shaft. X represents the primary shaft, on which are mounted the gear wheels A, B, C, and D. This primary shaft, as its name implies, is directly connected with the clutch shaft, and so takes the drive directly from the engine. Y is the secondary shaft, on which are mounted the gear wheels A1, B1, C1, and D1, and from the rear end of which the power is transmitted to the road wheels.

When the gear lever is in the neutral notch, all the gear wheels are out of mesh with each other, and consequently, although the engine revolves the shaft X, the power is not communicated to the shaft Y, which, provided the car is at rest, does not revolve. If, however, the car is running free, the turning of the road wheels will necessarily revolve the secondary shaft Y with its gear wheels.

Neutral to Low Speed—Now, taking it for granted that the car is at rest and the engine running, it is necessary, before the power can be communicated to the road wheels, that one of the gear wheels on the primary shaft X be moved into mesh with one of the gear wheels on the secondary shaft Y. Naturally, the low speed wheels will be the first to be brought into mesh. In other words, in order to start the car,

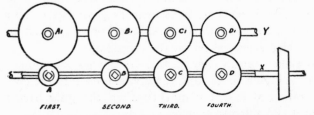

FIG. 1.—THE VARYING DIAMETERS OF THE WHEELS.

the very small wheel or pinion A will be moved into mesh with the very large wheel A1.

Now, the car being at rest, but the engine running, shaft Y (including wheel A1) will be motionless, but shaft X (including pinion A) will be revolving. If an attempt were made to get into the low speed while this condition of affairs existed, the teeth of A would grind against the teeth of A1. Consequently, the operator must take the clutch wholly out of engagement and wait a few moments until it has ceased revolving. Shaft X, and with it pinion A, will then have come to rest, and A and A1 can be brought into engagement with each other without grinding. (See Fig. 2.) Should the teeth come right opposite each other and refuse to engage, replace the gear lever in the neutral notch, let the clutch into engagement for the fraction of a second, and try again.

In getting into the reverse, the same programme should be followed.

It sometimes happens that the clutch shaft will not stop revolving when the clutch pedal is depressed. This is generally due to the clutch leather having swelled, or, in a plate or disk clutch, to the plates or disks sticking together. It may also be due to insufficient lubrication of the spigot bearing.

To change from neutral into the low speed or reverse is, under these circumstances, very difficult. The best plan is to slow the engine as much as possible, then suddenly close the throttle altogether, operate the gear lever, and then re-open the throttle before the engine has stopped revolving. The teeth of the gear wheels will probably grind a little, but

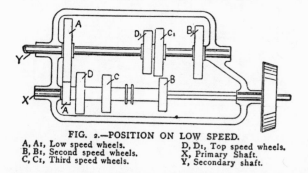

FIG. 2.—POSITION ON LOW SPEED.

A, A1, Low speed wheels.   D, D1, Top speed wheels.
B, B1, Second speed wheels.   X, Primary Shaft.
C, C1, Third speed wheels.   Y, Secondary shaft.

almost at the first touch the primary shaft, which, of course, is moving very slowly, will cease revolving, allowing the teeth to mesh. The condition of the clutch should be attended to at the first opportunity and the defect remedied.

From Low Speed to Second—To change from the low to the second speed, A must be taken out of engagement with A1, and B moved into engagement with B1. It will be noticed, however, that A is very much smaller than A1. Consequently, while A and A1 are in mesh, shaft Y (including wheel A1) will be revolving very much slower than shaft X (including pinion A). It will be also noticed that there is a considerable disparity between the sizes of wheels B and B1 (which must be brought into mesh for the second speed), though the difference is not so great as between A and A1. As already explained, however, it is essential, if a clean change is to be made, that the teeth of B and B1 should be moving approximately at the same speed when they are brought together. In other words, the speed of shaft X has to be reduced. (See Fig. 3.)

To accomplish this, the clutch must be sharply and wholly withdrawn just as A and A1 are taken out of mesh, and the gear lever moved gently into the second speed notch, so that there will be an appreciable interval in making the change, just sufficient and no more, to allow the shaft X, which is then disconnected from the clutch shaft, to slow down, so

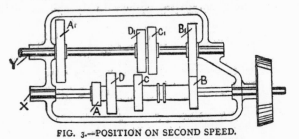

FIG. 3.—POSITION ON SECOND SPEED.

that the teeth of the two wheels are traveling at the same speed.

There are other factors, however, which complicate the movement, and render great judgment and experience necessary to effect an absolutely clean change. For example, if the car is running on the level when the clutch is withdrawn, the pace will not drop appreciably in the brief interval of time necessary for changing, and, consequently, the road wheels will continue to drive shaft Y at almost the same number of revolutions per minute as it was revolving before A and A1 were taken out of mesh. Under such circumstances, the actual movement of the gear lever forward need not take more time than about one second, if as much, the period depending to some extent on the weight of the clutch, and also the position of the throttle, for if it is comparatively open the engine will race when the load is taken off it, and, therefore, as the clutch comes out, it will start revolving faster. If, however, the car is running up a slight grade when the change is being made, it will lose speed more rapidly, and, consequently, it may require a slightly longer interval—a small fraction of a second longer, probably—to allow shaft X to slow down sufficiently to permit of B meshing cleanly with B1. Of course, if too long an interval is allowed, the car will have slowed down so much before the change is effected that the engine will not be able to pick up the higher gear.

On the other hand, if the car is running down-hill when the change is being made, it will increase in speed when the clutch is withdrawn, thus causing Y to revolve more rapidly

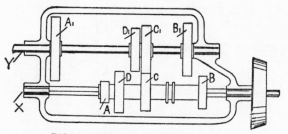

FIG. 4.—POSITION ON THIRD SPEED.

than before, and necessitating a less gradual change. The delay in moving the lever is in all cases, however, very slight. In fact, there need be no actual stop, but rather a gradual steady push forward. If the movement is too slow, the speed of shaft X will drop too much relatively to that of shaft Y, and the teeth of B and B1 will grind. It will then be necessary to let the clutch into engagement again for a fraction of a second so as to speed shaft X up a little, and to then continue the operation of pushing the change speed lever into the second speed notch.

Second to Third—In changing from second speed to third, the same procedure will have to be followed, but as we go up the scale the movement should be less gradual owing to the disparity in size between the primary and secondary gear wheels C and C1 (Fig. 4) being less, and consequently the difference in the speed of revolution of shafts X and Y will also be less.

Third to Fourth—In changing from the third to fourth speed, it is generally unnecessary to make any pause whatever, but to manipulate the lever with a quick, decisive motion, for in this case shaft X is not revolving much faster than shaft Y at the moment that C and C1 are taken out of mesh, and wheels D and D1 are of equal size. (See Fig. 5.)

If there is considerable friction between the male and female portions of the clutch so that it takes an appreciable time for the male portion to come wholly out of engagement, the slowing down of shaft X will take longer than otherwise.

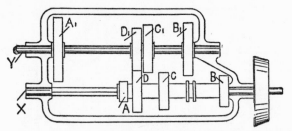

FIG. 5.—POSITION ON TOP SPEED.

If, however, there is a clutch stop fitted, shaft X will slow down very rapidly indeed, and the movement of the lever when changing up should be rapid.

Should the driver miss gear when changing up, he had better let the clutch into engagement for the fraction of a second, return to the gear he was on before, and then try again.

Changing Down—When changing down, the condition existing as to the relative speeds of shafts X and Y renders necessary a reversal of the operations. Starting with the fourth speed, it will be seen in the diagram that the gear wheels D and D1 are the same size. Sometimes D is bigger than D1—generally when a direct third speed is fitted. If D and D1 are the same size, shafts X and Y will revolve at the same speed, but if D is the bigger, X will revolve slower than Y. The third speed wheel C_1 will, of course, be revolving at the same speed as D_1. C, however, being a smaller wheel, will have to rotate quicker than C_1, to insure the teeth meshing, and consequently the shaft X will have to be quickened so as to enable these two wheels to mesh easily. The same applies to B and B_1 and A and A_1; but as the disparity in size is greater as lower speed gears are reached, the shaft X will have to be speeded up proportionately.

This speeding up of shaft X is accomplished by slipping the clutch—that is, by not taking it wholly out of engagement as when changing up, but by allowing the male portion to remain slightly in contact with the female. What is necessary is that the clutch should be so far withdrawn as to ease the pressure of the teeth against each other, so that the gears may be moved out of mesh. As soon as they come out of mesh, the clutch, still having a certain hold of the shaft, which is now free from the driving strain, rotates the latter at an accelerated speed owing to the engine automatically accelerating when the load is taken off.

The amount of slipping necessary can only be found by experience and experiment. As the different stages between high and low are reached, the disparity between the size of the gear wheels increases and, consequently, shaft Y has to be increasingly accelerated.

When changing into the reverse, the driver should be very careful not to attempt to make the change until the road wheels have come to rest. It is wise also to keep the clutch out, before making the change, sufficiently long to insure the primary shaft coming to rest.

We have dealt with the Panhard system because it is more simple to explain with it what is necessary in gear changing. In other gears, as in the case of the Mercedes type, in which a direct drive is obtained, and in which the power is transmitted to a countershaft and back to an extension of the primary shaft, exactly the same conditions obtain, and exactly the same methods of changing must be adopted.

If the countershaft in this case is regarded as the primary, which it practically is, it will be seen that it is in reality a Panhard type. In such cases, however, the direct top gear is easier to get into owing to it being accomplished by engaging some form of dog clutch instead of sliding wheels into mesh sideways.

So far we have dealt with general principles. There are other factors to be taken into consideration, however, such as the speed of the engine at the moment of changing and the variations in different designs. We shall deal with the engine speed first.

The Engine Speed as a Factor.

It will be easily understood that, if the engine is driving with the throttle open, or nearly open, as the clutch is withdrawn, the engine will race as the load has been taken off. Hence, there will be a brief period, at the moment when the male portion of the clutch is just coming out of engagement with the female, when the acceleration of the latter will cause a considerable increase in the revolution speed of the male portion, and, as the màle portion drives the shaft X, there will also be an increase of speed in the shaft X. This increase of speed will, needless to say, further increase the difficulty of making a clean change.

The exception to this is in the case of those gears which have a direct third speed and an indirect fourth speed; or where the secondary shaft is idle on the direct gear. In the former the car is geared up on the top speed, and, therefore, the operation of gear changing will be modified accordingly. In the latter case, changing gear from top to next gear will be rendered easier.

To obviate this difficulty, it is a common practice to take the foot off the accelerator, or operate the throttle lever, as the case may be, at the moment that the clutch is withdrawn, thus preventing the engine from racing when the load is taken off it. The moment the change of gear has been effected, it is necessary for the driver to push down the accelerator pedal again or operate the throttle lever without a moment's delay.

In some cases the clutch pedal is connected up to the throttle, and partly closes it when the clutch is withdrawn. On the level or down hill the closing of the throttle, and consequent slowing of the engine, works admirably, but on an up-grade it tends to reduce the power of the engine so much at a critical period that, unless the change is made very quickly and the throttle opened again with the least possible delay, the engine either picks up very slowly or else fails to pick up at all, so that when changing up on an ascent it may become necessary to drop back to the lower gear, or, when changing down, to drop a stage farther on to a still lower gear.

It is when changing up that the difficulty is greatest. As already explained, it is necessary that shaft X should be slowed, and that as quickly as possible, for every moment that elapses while the clutch is out the car is losing its momentum and slowing down. This slows down shaft Y (which was already traveling much slower than shaft X), consequently it adds still further to the difference between the speed of the two shafts. In other words, if shaft X accelerates abnormally at the moment the clutch is being withdrawn, it means a longer wait to allow it to slow, and during this longer wait Y is also steadily slowing down through the car losing its momentum. Hence, when the change is at last effected, the car has slowed so much that the engine may not be able to take up the drive, and one has to drop back again to the lower gear.

Also, there is another disadvantage. If the clutch is let in gradually when the engine is racing furiously, extreme friction will be generated which may burn the clutch leather. If it is let in suddenly, the strain on the engine and transmission systems will be enormous.

It will be seen, therefore, that there must not be undue delay when changing up on a hill, and that the engine must not be allowed to race furiously while the clutch is out.

The best practice is, immediately before changing, to throttle down to a point which would give in or about normal engine speed with the load off. Then change as rapidly as is possible without grinding the gear wheels, and just as the clutch is being let in again (but before it has fully engaged), open the throttle. The engine will then be accelerating again just as the male portion of the clutch is coming into frictional contact with the female, and unless the grade is too close to the limit of the gear it will pick up steadily, even when the full load comes on.

When changing down on an up-grade the difficulty is not so great. To insure a clean change, we want to increase the speed of shaft X as compared with shaft Y. The falling off in the momentum and speed of the car will assist towards this end by reducing the speed of Y. Consequently the engine can be run faster during the change when changing down than when changing up, especially if the clutch is only slipped slightly during the change; but, of course, the engine, and with it X, must not be accelerated too much. The change, as a rule, can be made fairly rapidly, and as the engine is running at a reasonably fast speed, it will pick up well.

On the level or down-hill the engine should always be throttled off, as under such circumstances there is no difficulty in picking up. The operator should be careful that the speed at which the car is traveling approximates to that to which he is about to descend, and, consequently, if he is changing on the level, for the sake of traffic or such like, he should first slow down the car by means of the throttle, or by taking the clutch out momentarily. In the latter case it facilitates changing to let the clutch into operation again for a fraction of a second, and declutch again slowly before effecting the change.

There is another system of changing down on a descent which works most satisfactorily, but requires some learning. With the throttle almost closed, take the clutch out of engagement, move the gears in operation out of mesh, but then pause with the gear lever between the two gears; next let the clutch in for a moment so as to speed up primary shaft X, declutch and change slowly into the lower gear. Under such circumstances, the car is likely to be traveling too fast for the lower gear, and, consequently, the clutch should be let into engagement very slowly or the car speed will be checked with a suddenness that will strain both engine and transmission.

The Use of the Brakes.

Nothing is more detrimental to a car than the improper and excessive use of the brakes. The driver should bear in mind that, no matter what system is adopted of checking speed—with the exception of the forces of gravity or inertia—a strain is brought to bear on the transmission system and tires, and that this strain becomes excessive and exceedingly detrimental if the car is checked or stopped with great suddenness. In most cases the engine itself forms a fairly efficient brake, and acts more smoothly and more gradually than is possible for any mechanical brake. For this reason it is less likely to cause side-slip. The best way, therefore, to stop a car is to gradually close the throttle, and the driver should begin to do so in ample time, so that the retarding influence may be as gentle and gradual as possible. To get the maximum stopping effect it is generally necessary to switch off the ignition, because very few throttles are so perfect in action that a certain amount of explosive mixture does not find its way through. In descending steep hills, however, the strain to the engine is considerable where this method of braking is solely employed, and consequently the rear wheel brakes should be used to assist the engine, for which purpose it is, of course, necessary that they should be disconnected from the clutch.

Some types of engine are so designed that the engine practically becomes an air compressor, and affords an exceedingly powerful and reliable form of brake. The pedal-regulated camshaft which attains this end should be gradually operated, and on steep hills the hind wheel brakes should be used to assist the engine.

As regards the hand and foot-applied brakes, all are agreed that one should be disconnected from the engine, and many experts consider that this should be done in the case of both. Of course under such circumstances it is very necessary to declutch by means of the clutch pedal when the car is being brought to an absolute standstill. These hand and foot-applied brakes should invariably be applied gradually, except in the case of a sudden and serious emergency. For general application, as in traffic for example, the foot-applied brake is the most convenient, but it causes the greatest amount of strain, owing to the braking effort being taken up through the transmission system. For this reason the rear wheel brakes should be used on all steep down-grades in preference to the countershaft brake, and great care should be observed to see that the compensating mechanism is in order, so that the retarding influence on one wheel is not greater than on the other.

The driver should train himself in the constant application of the hand brake, and he cannot do this better than by using the hand brake exclusively, say for a week at a time, so that he may instinctively be able to use this brake quickly in case of an emergency, instead of having to fumble clumsily for the lever. Needless to say, it is essential for safety that all brakes should be kept in perfect order, and it is a wise precaution to test them within the first few minutes after starting. There is no more hopeless position than to unexpectedly find one's brakes out of order when called upon to make a sudden stop.

Tapping in the Engine.

Sometimes it will be noticed that the engine, which has been running perfectly well and easily, will begin to make a slight tapping sound. It is not sufficiently pronounced to be called a knock, and very often it will puzzle the driver to know what it is caused by, and in the majority of cases he will be apt to put it down to some slight peculiarity of his valves. As a matter of fact, it is nothing of the kind, but is due to very slight premature ignition which is easily remedied.

One Cause of Irregular Firing.

If one's engine is heard to knock very violently, so much so that the first impression given is that either the crank-shaft has broken or the big end bearing bolts have got adrift, it is well before jumping at such a conclusion to carefully examine the ignition. In one such case which occurred at the end of a

Operating Devices—Locomobile.

The Jones Speedometer Odometer.

short tour, the engine started knocking so badly that the owner of the car feared to run it any further, and left it some thirty miles from home, wiring the makers that something had gone seriously wrong with the engine. It was ultimately discovered that the contact blade of the commutator was fractured and that the knock was due entirely to irregular firing caused thereby.

Want of Gasolene: Its Symptoms.

It is often a simple thing which causes an involuntary stop. This was brought home to a writer on the automobile press very forcibly on one occasion. The particular small car he was driving had the gasolene tank beneath the seat, and the supply to the carbureter was shut off by means of a needle valve. Through frequent use the thread of this valve had become sufficiently worn to enable the road vibrations to shake it round, and thus reduce the supply of gasolene. In the first place, he could not account for the extraordinary loss of power in the engine. Power rapidly decreased, and then firing back through the air inlet of the carbureter began to give additional trouble. When this stage was reached he considered it quite time to investigate matters. The first cause to which he attributed the trouble was bad inlet valves. These were examined, and found to be working quite correctly. He then tried starting the engine up, and it went at first turn, but very quickly repeated the previous performance, and back-fired through the carbureter. The next move was to examine the carbureter to see whether it was getting sufficient of the necessary fluid. It was found that the supply valve was very nearly closed, thus allowing only half the needful quantity of gasolene to pass to the carbureter.

Effect of Plunging Cars on the Carbureter.

When light, very easily sprung cars are driven with but one or two passengers on the front seat—the plunging of the cars over rough roads will be found to affect the gasolene feed to the float chamber of the carbureter. The plunging will cause the float to jump and flood or shut off the feed, so that for a few moments the engine is starved of gas. Next to weight on the back part of the car, this involuntary cutting out of the engine, when gasolene is fed by gravity, may be largely prevented by keeping the gasolene tank full. The head of gasolene appears considerably to check the undesirable action of the float when the car is plunging on bad roads.

To Avoid Sideslip Downhill.

Most owners have had experience of driving on frozen roads, and the novice will find, or has already found, that extreme precaution is necessary when descending winding hills. There is one practically safe method of descending without danger, and this applies, of course, to slippery roads of any kind in cities. It consists of driving with the wheels at one side in the gutter. If one wheel is already in the gutter, there is very little tendency for the car to slip out of it. Again, if the car is close to the sidewalk, a slip of an inch or two into the curbstone is not much to worry about. As long as one stays in the gutter it is impossible for the car to turn round and go broadside down the hill. Further, in many cases roads are only frozen on the crown, and at the side and in the gutter there is pretty good holding.

Luck and the Tire Bill.

Undoubtedly a very large item in the cost of running one's own car is that due to the upkeep of the pneumatic tires. This item varies very largely with different drivers of cars, and a low bill for tires is usually attributed to luck. Now, luck plays a very inconsiderable part in this respect; really and truly, one might say no part at all other than that of missing broken glass, horseshoe nails, etc. The most serious damage which is done to tires is that due to excessive speed, overloading, sudden letting in of the clutch, misuse of the brakes, and driving over newly paved roads with the full power of the engine operating at the road wheels. All of these are practically solely and entirely due to bad driving, and have nothing to do with inherent bad properties of the tire. With the flexible throttle control, as fitted to modern cars, the necessity of constantly applying brakes vanishes, and if only reasonable care is exercised by a driver, almost the whole of the running can be done on the throttle; hence the brake need only be used on very severe hills and for pulling up at any place. Some clutches are much fiercer in action than others, but the knack of gently letting in the clutch can be acquired if intelligently practiced, so that no snatch is transmitted from the engine to the road wheels. The sudden action of any clutch or brake simply causes lumps to be ripped from the tread of a tire when on a rough road and thus the life is very considerably reduced.

Another point is overloading the tire. The buyer of a car should insist upon having tires with an ample margin for the weight carried. The first cost may be a few dollars higher, but in the long run this is saved over and over again.

It should always be remembered that wet surfaces cut rubber much more readily than dry. In the case of small cuts on the tread these should at once be filled with one of the special tire repair preparations, to prevent them opening out or being further cut. If these remarks are properly digested, the tire bill will be considerably lessened apart from so-called luck.

Driving over Loose Stones.

A careful driver becomes much exercised as to how he may do his tires the least possible amount of harm when passing over a newly-laid patch of stones. The more general method is to drop down on to the bottom speed and go over as gently as may be, yet this oftentimes results in the tires being badly cut. Now, if when approaching a patch of loose stones the car is allowed to run right up to it at speed, and the clutch is taken out before the front wheels strike the stones, the vehicle will have sufficient momentum to carry it over most ordinary patches of new laid pavement at a minimum risk to the tires. If the momentum is insufficient to carry the car past the stones, nothing remains but to drop to the low speed and go on gently. On no account should the clutch be let in so that momentum may be maintained as immediately the engine begins to drive when the gear ratio speed is above that of the speed of the vehicle the very worst cutting action is put on the tires.

Driving Home on the Rim.

It must occasionally fall to the lot of every automobilist to find himself obliged to drive home on the rim—in other words, he is unable to keep any air in his tire, he is without spare tires or too short of time to struggle with a refractory inner tube, and so elects to drive on, and ignore the consequences. Common prudence will suggest a moderate speed, and if the distance to be traversed be short, the security bolts well tightened, and the road surface smooth, it is possible that little harm may be done. Supposing the cover to be badly burst, while the tube is in good condition bar the burst, it is a good plan to remove it and drive on the cover alone—its last drive most likely. If both cover and tube are in good order, and the deflation is due to a puncture or loose patch, it is well to screw the bolts up for all they are worth, and if the cause of puncture is to be found in the shape of a nail or piece of glass, remove it. When putting things right in the privacy of your garage you will doubtless find the leather heads of the security bolts badly crumpled; if they will straighten out so much the better, if not they can be made good with canvas. A most important point is to see that they are not bent out of shape as regards the plates which form the heads. These are in the form of a flat bottomed V, and the sides are very liable to spread under such treatment as suggested. If they are put back in such condition they fail to bed down into the rim, and in consequence the inner tube will be able to blow down under them, and give way at inconvenient times. Not that any time is convenient for tire trouble, but some times are less inconvenient than others.

Gear Missing in Speed Changes.

If, when changing speed, the gear misses, depress the clutch pedal again quickly, and the gears will invariably come in at once without causing any jar upon them. When firmly in, the clutch should be let in gently to pick up the momentum the car has lost.

Engine Thumping at Gear Changes.

Sometimes when a gear change from a lower to a higher speed has been made, it will be found that the engine commences to thump heavily. This is due to the fact that the change has been made a little too soon and before the speed of the car or the resistance warranted it. The thumping can be instantly stopped by lightly touching the clutch pedal, so that a little slip takes place. The engine then quickly picks up, and the thumping ceases.

Epicyclic Gear Changing.

Owners of cars with epicycloidal change speed gearing should be particularly careful to change their gears gently. As a matter of fact, the amateur driver who is used to sliding gear changing is, for a short time, hopelessly at sea on a car with the type of gear mentioned, for whereas with the sliding gear a quick motion is necessary for gear changing, the other type requires a gradual feeling action for the change. Thus, on cars employing epicyclic gears, the driver should be careful to apply the brake which changes the gear as gradually as possible, otherwise the strain on the gear is very considerable, and stripping a by no means distant possibility. Lubrication of the drums is quite permissible, and is usually provided for, but if not, the driver of the car should see that some thin oil is used occasionally to grease the peripheries of the various speed-changing brake drums.

Returning to the Slow Speed Gear.

When one has run up to and come to a rest at a point at which it is desired to stop on top speed, a little difficulty will sometimes be found in returning the change speed lever to the neutral notch in the quadrant. The teeth of the toothed wheels on the sliding sleeve on the clutchshaft do not at the moment exactly coincide with the gaps in the toothed wheels on the gearshaft, and the wheels will not pass each other. Of course, the clutch can be let in slightly, which would alter their position with regard to each other, but not infrequently the teeth still foul. The depression of the brake pedal, however, and the consequent grip of the brake bands, or blocks, on the brake drum will, permitted by the slight play in the propeller-shaft, cause the gearshaft to move just enough to permit the passage of the wheels on the sliding sleeve through their fellows, and allow the neutral notch to be at once attained.

To Learn Changing Gear.

This can be done in the garage or anywhere private. Block up the rear axle well and solidly, so that the tires are at least two inches from the ground level, and wedge the front wheels at front and back, with substantial wedges or planks. Start up the engine again, and sit at the steering wheel seat; depress the clutch pedal slightly, and gently work the speed lever to try and bring it into the first speed notch. Probably a grating noise will be heard, and you may fail to get the wheels properly in mesh. Let back the lever to its original position and try again. If the lever goes into the notch, then at once let up the clutch pedal gently, and you will notice the rear wheels will at once commence to revolve. Depress the clutch and they will stop; let it in again and they start. Practice this, and afterward try to get in the next speed higher, first by depressing the clutch, and at the same instant bring the speed lever into the next higher notch, and immediately let the clutch in gently without loss of time. The rear wheels will now revolve faster, and you can then try higher speeds; then practice reducing the gear by doing everything in the same order. While on each of the gears, the engine can be run fast or slow with the throttle and spark levers, as before mentioned. The reverse can then be tried exactly in the same manner, most cars having the reverse and forward speeds actuated by means of one lever. In the exceptions to this rule there is no difficulty in following out the operations to be gone through if the levers are carefully examined and their effect noted when they are operated.

Never Look at the Lever Quadrant.

One occasionally comes across car owners of some experience—men, too, who profess to be particularly keen upon mastering the technique of their machines—who have not acquired such rudimentary skill as is involved in changing gears without looking down to see when the lever is alongside a notch in the quadrant. It may be excusable for absolute beginners to do this, but it is an extremely dangerous practice when driving in traffic to take one's eyes from the road in order to look down at the quadrant when changing gears. Particularly at night time should the practice be avoided, so that the dodge of rigging up an electric lamp in a position where it will illuminate the quadrant must be regarded as the invariable sign of the clumsy beginner. Gear should be changed by feeling, not by sight. The only time the quadrant should be looked at is when one has stopped on the top speed. One should then see that the lever has been put in the neutral notch before leaving the car.

Driving on the Brake.

It is very bad practice to drive on the brake, though some people who know no better think it showy. By driving on the brake we mean driving jerkily. For instance, we will assume that the driver is coming to a turn or overtaking a block in the traffic. Instead of reducing his speed gradually as soon as he sees the necessity for a slack or perhaps a stop, he rushes up to the point, and then jams on all his brakes and pulls his car up dead. The next moment, as the necessity for the slack has passed, he crowds on all available power without allowing his engine a moment to recover and introduce itself gradually to its car. This sort of thing ruins any engine and car, as it subjects them to extremely severe shocks and strains. In fact, there is no doubt whatever that more than one mysterious failure has been caused by the parts being overstrained through this reprehensible manner of driving.

Using the Brakes.

The fact that there are two or more brakes to every car seems to have escaped the notice of many drivers, for in a large proportion of cases the hand brake is used solely as a sort of stand-by. The foot brake is always used, the hand brake rarely, with the result that the first is unduly worn, while the wheel drums are hardly ever called into play. Now, apart from the fact that this is not economy, it is very bad driving policy, in that the driver, never using his hand brake, does not cultivate the instinctive operative faculty, with the result that in cases of urgent need thought is necessary before he can apply his emergency brake. Now, on many of the old pattern cars this was perhaps excusable, for the lever was frequently very awkward to reach and cumbrously unhandy. On the newer cars, however, this has been altered. In many cases, the hand brake lever is pivoted to and swings over a parallel quadrant to that for the change-speed lever, and it is generally in convenient reach of the driver.

The Rational Method of Braking.

Beyond this, many makers have gone a step further, and so arranged that their brake lever pulls back towards the driver, in place of the older push-forward motion. This is the rational action, since, should it be necessary to apply the whole braking power the car possesses, the driver would be pushing with his feet and pulling with his hand, each force exerted transferring its reaction to the other brake, thus rendering the motions both more efficient and more natural. With almost all wheel brakes, compensating devices are fitted, so that the retarding action on each wheel is the same, and all the strain is taken by the hub of the wheel. Where the countershaft brake or brakes or the propeller-shaft brake is used, there is all the slack in the chains or the lash in the teeth to be taken up before the action takes place, or, in other words, there is a reversal of strain from the brake backward. If you want your car to last, use the hand brake for ordinary driving more widely. It is only a question of use. Use is second nature, and the cultivation of the hand brake may save the automobilist a serious accident. In the interests of public safety also every driver should accustom himself to the instant use of all his available braking power.

Driving on Treacherous Roads.

Those who are unfamiliar with the gyrations of a motor car under the influence of sideslip are often at a loss to know what to do when the car begins to slip even in a gentle manner. Now, as a matter of fact, sideslip is one of those things which come upon one suddenly; but if a number of such sideslips are analyzed they will be found to be due to a too harsh application of the brakes, or to the upward changing of the gears, when the conditions are such as not to permit of the road wheels taking up the increased speed applied to them and at the same time getting a firm grip of the road. As a general rule, it will be found, if one drives on one's proper side of the road, that the tendency of the car is to slip towards the off or right-hand side, this being due to the camber of the road, so that the rear wheels of the car have an inclination to slide upon the greasy surface down to the gutter. On some of the narrow and highly cambered roads occasionally met with there is the greatest difficulty experienced in keeping the car straight. The natural inclination is for it to proceed crab fashion rather than in a straight line.

Conduct in Sideslip.

Under such circumstances it is perhaps better to wait until the way is clear, when the car can be put directly across the road and again brought on to the crown, when all will go well so long as the crown of the road is kept to. Under other circumstances, when the car shows an inclination to slip towards the right, if the front wheels are also steered towards the right they have a wholesome checking influence upon the rear wheels, which, once having commenced to slide, prefer to take the front wheels as a pivot whereon to turn, and if the pace or the weight of the car and the general conditions are such as to give sufficient momentum, it is not at all unusual for the car to turn completely round. In such instances the checking influence of the front wheels is not very great, but is frequently sufficient to prevent the car doing any serious damage to itself. If, on the other hand, the wheels are turned outward, they only aggravate the sideslip by causing the driving wheels to push the front of the car more up on to the crown of the road, so giving sufficient momentum at the rear end either to turn the car itself completely round, or possibly to damage the rear wheels or axles seriously by a violent collision with the curb.

Starting under Difficulties.

If an engine will not start on the switch, and the starting handle is lost or so bent through a collision as to be useless, the car may be pushed with the engine in gear, or even jacked up at the back. This plan has been tried occasionally when a back wheel was turned by hand, which, of course, made the engine work. Directly it fires, the speed lever must be put into the neutral position and the jack removed. This operation, however, needs care, particularly when the car has a chain drive.

A few cars are still used with detachable starting handles, and these, like any other articles, can be lost. If the engine will start on the switch, the problem of getting a car under way is easily solved. Another alternative is to put the car in gear and get a person to push the car. If, however, one has no passengers, and there is nobody at hand to give assistance, the difficulty is one which might be thought to be insurmountable.

We give one method suggested for overcoming the difficulty, but which should not be put into practice unless everything else fails.

One rear wheel should be jacked up, and everything set for starting. The jacked-up wheel should now be pulled round in a forward direction, which will rotate the engine. The top gear should be put into engagement, as the engine will then start with less manual effort. Directly the engine is rotated, the speed lever should be put into the neutral gear position, before the jack is removed.

Starting a Motor on Coal Gas.

When attempting to start a gasolene engine "from the cold," instead of injecting gasolene into the cylinders or warming the carbureter with hot cloths, insert one end of a piece of rubber gas tubing in the air intake of carbureter, and connect the other end of tube to the nearest gas bracket. Upon turning on the gas, the engine will be found to go off at the first or second turn of the starting handle, and, unless it be of very large dimensions or the gas supply very attenuated, will continue to run at a moderate speed. Gasolene can now be turned on, the carbureter flooded, and, after a few seconds, the gas turned off, leaving the engine running on gasolene. This method will be found very simple in practice, and saves much exertion at the starting handle. When an engine is missing fire, it can readily be ascertained by running the engine on coal gas as described above, whether the carbureter is at fault or not.

One word of caution: Owing to the strong suction in the air intake, the coal gas is sucked out of the gas main much faster than it would issue by its own pressure, and the result is that any lights in the vicinity will probably be sucked out.

Popping in the Muffler.

Numerous owners who have learned to drive a De Dion car, enquire how to account for explosions in the exhaust-box, and how they can be prevented. One such owner says that the engine must be bewitched, inasmuch as it nearly always pops when passing restive horses. The explanation is simple, and the cure of the phenomenon easy. Popping in the muffler nearly always occurs through the mixture being too weak, so that the charge is not exploded in the cylinder, but passes out through the exhaust-valve into the muffler, where it is ignited by the heat of the exhaust pipe or box. When traveling fast, the mixture lever is adjusted to admit plenty of air to the carbureter; in the De Dion car the mixture lever is pushed toward the steering column, while the timing lever is pushed forward for early sparking; but when the pace is suddenly checked, as it naturally would be when approaching a restive horse, the mixture is upset because the piston speed is not sufficiently great to suck in a sufficiency of spray to mingle with the air; thus it happens that the very act of suddenly checking the car in order to pass a restive horse slowly has the effect of provoking explosions. The remedy is always to remember to push the mixture lever forward when suddenly checking speed.

Gasolene Leakage: Lamp Dangers.

If a leak in the gasolene tank or connections is discovered at night, the lamps should be put out at once, and care taken that no light is brought near the car. If it is impossible to rectify the leak without light, and no electric lamp or torch is available, the acetylene lamp may be lighted and placed at least four yards from the car. When the leak is stopped, the escaped gasolene should be wiped away, and a few minutes should be spent in waiting for what is left to evaporate before attempting to light the lamps.

Driving with Slack Chains.

"It once fell to our lot to drive a light car having side chain drive," writes an early enthusiast in motoring. "These chains were so loose as to cause some anxiety, for there was every possibility of their leaving the sprockets. This eventually happened, but luckily gave no great trouble in replacement. It was found that the stretcher bars had been lengthened out to their utmost, and, therefore, there was no chance of giving the chains the necessary adjustment; and being well on into the night, it was hardly a pleasant task to start taking a link out of both chains. To prevent further possibility of the chain coming off, we religiously stuck to the second gear for the remainder of our journey—some sixteen or eighteen miles— and drove on the brake when descending hills. The object of this was to keep the chain taut on its top side, with the engine throttled down and the brake just applied sufficiently to re- tard the car to keep the chain in the desired position, and this prevented all further troubles."

Extemporizing a Valve Spring.

A useful addition to the motorist's outfit is a length of piano wire about the same gauge as the existing inlet spring. It not infrequently happens that a proper valve spring is not included in the spare parts carried, and when one of these becomes weakened or breaks, it is often a matter of difficulty to get even so small a thing into proper working order again. By carrying a piece of wire of this type, a spring of practically any required strength can be made and used without the necessity of tempering, as would be the case with most of the other kinds of wire used for spring making. This may appear to some to be superfluous, but many owners have had experiences in which a length of wire would have meant a great saving of time and temper had it been available.

Hauling a Car.

In the event of a breakdown irremediable upon the road, when recourse must be made to haulage by another car, or anything that can exert tractive force, care should be taken as to the manner in which the tow rope is attached to the car. It is by no means advisable to make the tow rope fast to the front axle; it is better to secure it to the projecting ends of the frame, which serve as spring horns, and pass the rope between these and the ends of the springs themselves. The haulage stress is then distributed evenly through the frame to both axles. The ends of the rope so passed should be taken and attached to any suitable part of the haulage equipment. If the car is to be loaded up on to a dray or wagon, take care that the wheels of the dray are securely blocked before any attempt is made to run the car up the inclined planks by which the floor of the dray is to be gained. Be ready also with suitable blocks or rods to secure the wheels of the car and arrest it at any part of the ascent if this should prove necessary from any cause whatever. Where a car has sustained such damage to one of the front wheels that it cannot travel on it, a strong pole may be passed under the front axle or the frame, and fastened to the back axle. The front end of the pole can then be attached to the towing vehicle, so that the damaged wheel is raised just off the ground.

Steering with Broken Gear.

Happily, steering gears are not now so prone to give way as they were a few years ago, but should any reader be so unfortunate as to have a distance rod of the steering gear come adrift, the following tip may be of use: Failing any temporary repairs, the car should be turned round by manual aid, and the front wheel which is not connected to the steering wheel should be lashed up to prevent its turning athwart the car. The vehicle may now be driven slowly backward, steering by the one wheel, which now becomes a trailer. This method is, of course, bad for the tire, and should only be resorted to when a repair can be effected within a couple of miles or so.

Economizing Gasolene.

The distance which one driver can accomplish on a given quantity of gasolene is often a subject of much astonishment to the driver of another and similar car, who finds it almost impossible to get the same results out of his own vehicle, although it is, as we have remarked, identical with the one consuming the lower quantity. The whole question lies in the fact that the one who is able to use a lower quantity of gasolene has hit upon the correct method of running his engine—and that is allowing the carbureter to take in as much air as it possibly can, and still to retain a good mixture. The most effective mixture of spirituous vapor and air is that which will run the engine at its highest power, which power is in no way increased by increasing the richness of the mixture. What is really meant by this can easily be ascertained by the owner of any motor in the following manner: Close down the air opening to the carbureter so as to obtain a rich mixture for starting, and then turn the starting handle, when the motor commences to work. Attention should now be turned to the air inlet. Open this slowly, and if a governor is fitted this should previously have been put out of action by the accelerator being pulled up or tied down, as the case may be. As the mixture assumes its better proportion, the engine will perceptibly quicken its speed, and with its speed the power, of course, increases. Continue opening the air inlet until it is wide open, and if there is no marked diminution in the speed of the engine, it may be assumed that it is running on the best proportion of mixture obtainable. If, on the other hand, the engine begins to slow down, the air inlet should be closed down again until the engine picks up its previous speed and gives out that note which spells power. The engine is now running to its best advantage, and is consuming the smallest amount of gasolene possible. At the same time this is only a rough guide to getting the correct adjustment, as the engine is doing no work. A road trial must be made to see how nearly the garage ideal can be reached. This applies to the vast majority of carbureter adjustments.

Contributory Causes of Loss of Power.

From time to time one comes across motors of which their owners complain that, while they do very well on the level, they behave scandalously when a hill of any gravity presents itself before them. Making a general and cursory test, it is found that the compression in each cylinder is good, the ignition apparently satisfactory, the timing correct, the operation of the valves visually good—in fact, there seems nothing emphatically responsible for the sluggishness of which the owner complains. Now, there is only one thing to do in such case, and that one comprises many. It is to go carefully and minutely through the motor, and, though it will not be found that any one detail is radically at fault, yet it is more than probable that one or more sparking plugs are dirty or have spark gaps too large, the electrical connections are somewhere loose and dirty, there is a slight short somewhere, there is deposit in the carbureter, or the gauze filters at the bottom of the tank or in the union close to the float feed chamber are more or less choked, an exhaust spring is weak and its valve does not close as smartly as it should, the holes in the muffler are choked with mud or grease and there is some back pressure caused thereby, one of the brakes is rubbing more or less on its drum, a pneumatic tire is soft, the accumulators are down a bit, or there is a considerable deposit of carbon on the combustion chamber walls and piston heads. These small matters taken separately do not appear to be particularly serious, and should not of themselves detract in any marked degree from the pulling power of the engine. Let us suppose, however, that each of these little failings reduces the horse-power by one-tenth. It will easily be seen that their sum total of reduction is enough, and more than enough, to deprive the engine of that vim without feeling which no true automobilist is truly happy at the wheel.

Substitute for a Governor.

Single-cylinder cars, and, in fact, most of the less expensive ones, are somewhat difficult to drive in traffic. The constant manipulation of the clutch necessitates frequent acceleration or slowing down of the engine. This is generally done by keeping the hand on the advance spark lever, so that when the clutch is taken out this is moved back to slow the engine down on running light. On letting the clutch in again, the spark is advanced to enable the engine to give the required power for driving. For these operations two hands are necessary—one on the steering wheel and one on the sparking lever. If, in addition, it is necessary to change speed rapidly, or to use the hand brakes, either the steering wheel must be let go altogether or the engine must be allowed to race—that is, if it is not fitted with a governor of some kind. This partly applies to speed changing. When changing up, the engine has to be slowed from the moment the clutch is withdrawn until the higher gear and clutch are engaged, when the spark can be advanced. If this is not done, the moment the clutch is depressed as a preliminary to gear changing, the engine races objectionably.

A simple way to overcome the difficulty is to connect the clutch pedal to the contact breaker, so that when the clutch pedal is depressed to withdraw the clutch the sparking is retarded, but allowed to return immediately the clutch is re-engaged. This is done by disconnecting the contact breaker from its advance spark lever, and fitting a spring tending to advance it to its utmost. A wire or rod is then fitted from the contact breaker to the usual control lever, enabling it to be set in any position by pulling it back by means of the hand lever against the action of the spring. This leaves the contact breaker controllable in exactly the same manner as before. From the clutch pedal or some part of the clutch connections a wire is led to the contact breaker in such a way as to pull it back to its most retarded position when the clutch pedal is fully depressed. This can best be done by means of wires, though they are somewhat unreliable; if rods are used, a sliding connection must be made between the clutch rod and hand lever rod to allow the contact breaker to be retarded by the clutch rod without necessitating any movement of the hand lever.

Starting Single-cylinder Engines.

In starting single-cylinder engines, very often trouble is experienced, this apparently being due to the engine being cold or to the carbureter hardly giving a correct mixture. With a De Dion type of engine, this trouble is readily got over by simply leaving the ignition switch off, and then depressing the inlet valve, and at the same time giving about three or four brisk turns to the crankshaft. Then when the switch is placed in the on position and the crankshaft given a brisk jerk so as to bring the piston over the compression point, it will be found that starting is quite easy. Of course, the throttle valve must be opened before the inlet valve is depressed.

How to Get the Best Work Out of a Motor.

Here are three good fundamental rules for getting the best work with the least consumption out of your engine:

1. Drive with ignition advanced to the utmost short of engine knock.

2. Admit as much air to the carbureter as possible short of getting misfires.

This, of course, only obtains with carbureters in which the air supply is controllable.

3. Never let the engine run hot or in want of the proper supply of lubricating oil.

To Start an Engine Easily.

One often hears of motorists, especially novices, who have great difficulty in starting up their engines. They are often afraid to stop their engines while leaving the car for a few minutes, on account of their difficulties on re-starting. In most cases starting is quite easy if care is taken always to close the additonal air inlet and open the throttle fully. If necessary, the carbureter should be flooded slightly. This should be done not by lifting the needle valve, or by holding down the plunger, as in a Longuemare carbureter, but by lifting and depressing it sharply, so as to spray the gasolene from the jet right up the inlet pipe. This coats the walls of the pipe with gasolene, and a firing mixture is taken into the engine at once, no matter how slowly it is turned over. The starting handle should always be turned round sharply through the three easy strokes, so as to insure sufficient suction to take in a proper mixture, and should then be jerked over the compression stroke by an upward pull on the handle. With carbureters of the Longuemare type, in which the inlet is at right angles to the jet, if the carbureter be flooded too much, an excess of gasolene collects in the well at the bottom of the jet, and far too rich a mixture is obtained for starting. For this reason excessive flooding should always be avoided, as it is rarely, if ever, successful in getting the engine under way. A good tip to facilitate starting is to open the throttle wide and close the air inlet just before switching off, so that the cylinders and inlet pipe are filled with a rich mixture, ready for the first spark on turning the engine over. Some drivers always make a point of starting up with the left hand, so that in the event of a back-kick the right hand gets off scot free, though there is no occasion for anybody receiving a bad back-kick. However, it is as well to cultivate the habit of starting up with the left hand, so that should the driver experience a sprained wrist, he can get along by using the other hand. It will be found easier if on putting the car away for the night the gasolene cock is turned off before the engine is stopped, and the carbureter will then become empty without the trouble of drawing the gasolene off. In very cold weather it will be found helpful to fill up with warm water, thereby warming the engine, which will then start at the first or second turn.

To Prevent Being Dazzled.

It is always advisable to have ready a pair of tinted or smoked glasses or goggles, so as to be prepared for driving against a low sun. In the early morning, and less frequently in the evening, when one is driving facing a low sun, it is quite impossible to see. If a pair of smoked glasses are available, there is no difficulty. Of course, the trouble only occurs when one is driving almost directly against the sun, and without tinted glasses it is quite impossible to proceed with safety either to oneself or to other road users, at anything above a mere crawl. There have been many horse and cycle accidents, some of them fatal, entirely due to the blinding effect of a low sun.

For Stopping Leaks.

Always carry a piece of bread somewhere on your car, says a practical French motorist; rye bread for choice. Rye bread is sometimes difficult of acquisition in this country, so a good wheat bread may suffice. The bread is not to be stored against a prolonged "panne" (i. e., "trouble"), and consequent famine in the depth of the wilds, but because under certain circumstances the staff of life can be of much avail in directions other than that of alimentation. A slight leak in a radiator can be most efficiently, although temporarily, staunched by means of paste made from bread kneaded with the fingers. The paste must be well kneaded, then spread over the leaky part, and worked in with some tool which will do duty as a spatula, just in the way painters work up their colors on a palette.

Attention to Tire Valve and Bolt Nuts.

After every run out on a car, the air tube valve nut and also all the securing bolt nuts should be carefully gone over to feel whether they have worked slack. With the running on the road this frequently happens, so that it is a good plan to try all of these with a small pair of pliers, as the thumb and finger grip on these is not sufficient to tighten them up satisfactorily. If the bolt nuts are allowed to get slack, there is a great tendency to shear the bolts or deform their heads. The heads tend also to tip up, and the result is that the inner tube gets nipped beneath the head, and in a very short time bursts, thus causing serious trouble on the road, but the pliers must be used very lightly.

Skidding or Side-slip.

Skidding is one of the most dangerous enemies that the automobilist has to guard against. There would seem to be no law governing side-slip, and at times no amount of skill in driving will entirely prevent it, though the danger may be modified to an extent. Skidding may be divided into two classes:

1. Due to grip of road surface being insufficient to enable driving wheels to propel car. In this case, as the road friction is not likely to be the same under each driving wheel, the differential enables that wheel having the better hold to do more than its share of propelling, with the result that the car is slewed round out of its course. This is the form of skid which is easiest to correct, for it is only necessary to take the clutch out.

2. Due to either change of direction of car or reduction of its speed under conditions when road surface is slimy and treacherous. This class of side-slip has huge possibilities and can only be avoided by driving slowly or, in fact, as if all brakes on the car had been dismantled. Carefully watch the way in which the road happens to dish, especially round corners. Of course with non-skid chains or bands these difficulties mostly vanish, but it must be remembered that a man who has never learnt to drive without such devices becomes

hopelessly lost if he happens to be driving a car having tires with ordinary treads on a slippery road. Apart from bad road surface, skidding is promoted by a faulty differential, back brakes unequally adjusted, frame or axles being out of alignment, or one tire having slightly greater diameter than its fellow.

The class of mud on which a motor car slips is exactly the same as that which affects a bicycle, and consequently the driver who is also a cyclist will be in a better position to judge than one who is not. Briefly, if the mud is thick and half dried, or if there is a thin film of grease over the paving, or if the road surface is composed of a slimy quality of limestone, the driver must exercise great caution. Frozen roads are, as a rule, safe. A sheet of ice, however, must be traversed cautiously, and if the surface has sufficiently thawed to become wet, it will be even more treacherous than the worst class of mud.

The best safeguard against side-slipping is to travel slowly at a steady, uniform pace. A sudden, violent application of the brakes, a sharp turn of the steering wheel or a sudden acceleration of pace may set up slipping. The driver should therefore, try to run his engine at an absolutely uniform speed, and should avoid traveling at a pace which would necessitate a strong application of the brakes should an obstruction suddenly block the road. In fact, when the grease is really bad, he should regulate his speed so that the manipulation of the throttle lever will slow the car sufficiently to provide for the ordinary exigencies of traffic.

The action of a car on a greasy or slippery road is often deceptive. The driver may find he can maintain a fast pace without any sign of side-slip, but he is almost helpless should he need arise for a sudden stop. If he puts the brakes on suddenly, the car may swing right round. A swerve or an attempt to take a corner quickly will also have the same effect.

When a side-slip does occur, the driver should declutch the engine on the moment. If he has applied his brakes, he should let them off again, and should momentarily give the car its head, so as to afford the wheels an opportunity of biting, but should then instantly turn the steering wheel in the direction necessary to right the car. If the wheel is violently turned in the opposite direction to the slip, the car is most likely to continue slipping, and perhaps will turn completely round Should the latter happen, the driver must let his clutch in again, at the very moment that the front of the car points directly up or down the road, when the front wheels will probably again grip.

There is practically no time to think in the case of a side slip. The necessary action is instinctive and practically instantaneous. If the driver does not declutch at once the car will dive into the ditch, and if he does not do the right thing at the right moment with the steering wheel the car will turn round. He will only gain skill by experience, and the only way to avoid accident while gaining the necessary skill is to drive very slowly at first, so that if a slip occurs which he is unable to control no damage will result. It is a good plan to practice side-slipping at a slow pace on a wide, unfrequented road. The control will then come very quickly. A really expert driver is able to actually reverse his direction by a sudden twist of the steering wheel, and yet control the slip so that the car will "fetch up" when it assumes an end-on position in the roadway.

When descending a steep hill the dangers resulting from side-slip are intensified, for the brakes cannot be safely used to any extent, and the car may continue sliding broadside on or slowly revolving owing to the slope of the hill. On an exceptionally slippery hill, as, for example, when the surface is coated with wet ice, a safe descent may often be effected by driving with the wheels at one side in the gutter. This gives the wheels a bite, and tends to prevent the car swinging broadside on. Also if a slip does occur the proximity of the curb be it of earth or stone, prevents serious results should the car strike sideways and come to an immediate stop.

It may, perhaps, seem that driving on a greasy road is exceedingly dangerous. To the experienced driver, however, it is not so. He quickly learns the speed at which he can travel with safety, and the amount to which the brakes can be applied without causing side-slip. Should the car swing round, it will not sustain any damage unless it strikes some obstruction or glides into a ditch.

There are many non-skid devices on the market of more or less efficiency, by the use of which the risk is reduced to a minimum.

THE ART OF DRIVING.

Having dealt with the manipulat on of the clutch and the various control levers so as to get the best results out of the car, we shall now give some hints on how to become a safe and expert driver. The beginner too often falls into the mistake of thinking that to drive a car well is a very simple matter, and before he has found out his mistake he may have caused injury through faulty manipulation, and perhaps have met with a more or less serious accident. He should take as his motto, *"Festina lente"* (Hasten slowly), and should not conclude that because he can steer straight on a clear road, it is therefore safe to travel fast. Nothing but experience will teach him to act instinctively in an emergency, and until he can so act he is in constant and imminent danger if he attempts to drive fast. He must bear in mind also, that a motor car requires almost as much sympathy as a horse if the best results are to be attained.

His initial practice should be done at a very slow speed, not more than from 10 to 15 miles an hour. He should learn how to slow, to stop, to reverse and to turn, and should practice these various operations until he is perfect. As regards steering, he should not be satisfied until he is able to follow a true course, and if, on descending a steep hill for example, the steering should show a tendency to get out of control and the car to sway, he should not lose his head and jam on his brakes, but should check the car gradually by means of the throttle until he has coaxed it into the way of rectitude once more. Even with drivers who have had some little experience, this danger of a swing from side to side being set up is one that has to be reckoned with.

To slow down gradually, use the throttle; to stop altogether, check the pace by the same means, but when the car has dropped to a speed of a few miles an hour, declutch and apply the hand-brake. To stop in an emergency, declutch and apply both brakes, but only to an extent that is absolutely necessary.

Ascending Hills.

When approaching a hill, it is often well to rush it, if the coast is clear. For this purpose advance the ignition, open the throttle, and temporarily race the engine. The momentum will carry the car .up a considerable way. As the engine slows, gradually retard the ignition, and the moment the engine shows any signs of laboring, change on to the next speed. As the engine picks up under the lighter load, the ignition can be slightly advanced again, so as to get the best results out of it. It is a bad practice to *frequently* slip the clutch in order to struggle over the crest of the hill without changing. When climbing on the low speed it is a mistake to race the engine— taking it for granted that the gradient is well within the car's powers. Racing is very severe on the engine under such circumstances, and will cause overheating.

Descending Hills.

In descending hills, both judgment and experience are necessary. If the grade is gentle and the road straight, free from traffic, and without side roads, a fast pace may be maintained. Under no circumstances, however, should a steep hill be descended fast if there are blind turns or if there is much traffic about. On dangerously steep down-grades it is essential to safety to begin the descent slowly. At a fast speed the momentum is enormous, and once the car has got out of control the brakes cannot be relied upon to hold it. Most of the serious accidents recorded have been due to drivers tackling a dangerous hill at too fast a pace and losing control. If the driver, through want of caution, finds himself traveling too fast on a dangerous descent, he should act promptly but with discretion. To jam the brakes on to their fullest may only cause one or both to collapse. Taking it for granted that he is running against compression (with the ignition switched off), he should apply both brakes with gradually increasing pressure until the speed is checked, and should descend the rest of the hill at a slow speed, relying upon compression and one of the brakes, using these alternately, so that they will not overheat, and keeping the other in reserve. If one brake is connected to the clutch, of course he can only use the other in combination with the engine. At a high speed the engine compression loses a large proportion of its effectiveness, and it may then become necessary for him to apply the second brake, thus declutching. The operation should be done quickly, but with judgment. On a long hill, which is steep, but not necessarily dangerous, it is very unwise to descend at a high speed with the brakes on. The heat generated under such circumstances is enormous, and the brakes at any moment may become ineffective, or even collapse, when, with the high momentum obtained, it would be impossible to stop the car. On long, gentle hills it is advisable to switch off, as this gives the engine a chance of cooling. Very few throttles are absolutely gastight.

When surmounting an exceptionally steep incline, on, say, the low speed, it is well to keep in view the possibility of a shaft breaking or a chain coming off, when probably the only available brakes, namely those on the back wheels, might not prove strong enough if the car commenced to run backward. A good plan is to hug the near side of the road (if not a precipice) so that if such an accident occurred the car should be quickly backed into the curb, fence or gutter. If the road is wide, however, hug the most dangerous side, and then, in case of a stoppage from the above causes, swing right across the road backward. The car will probably come to a standstill before touching the curb or fence.

Driving in Public Streets.

Exhibition driving in the public streets is at least bad style. It should be remembered that there are many people who are unable to judge how quickly your car can stop, and though it may be distinctly humorous to see an elderly person dancing a fandango in front of a car which has some time previously come to rest, there is no doubt that much needless irritation and dislike for automobiles in general may be thus caused.

If, in traffic driving, a doubt arises as to who should give way, be sure to do so yourself. Doubts of this nature gradually become fewer as a driver's experience and judgment increase.

On Turning Corners.

The art of taking corners without endangering oneself and other road users is worth cultivating. The motorist should make an invariable habit of keeping to his own side of the road at these corners, even though, as when turning to the left, the act of swinging wide will bring him off the crown of the road and necessitate a slower pace. When turning to the right, he should not take the corner at such a speed as will make him swing wide, for if other traffic is advancing to meet him, an accident is very likely to occur. The slower the corner is taken, the less will be the strain on his differential gear and tires. For this reason also it is very advisable to declutch as the car begins to turn, and not let the clutch into engagement again until the corner has been almost negotiated. Another important point should be borne in mind, and that is, that the severe application of the brakes when in the act of turning a corner tends to upset the car, and, if for this reason alone, the corner should not be taken fast.

Passing Side Roads.

Side roads constitute a very serious danger, especially if the fences are so high as to obscure the view. If the automobilist is on the main road he should sound his horn and slow down on approaching the side road. His safest position under such circumstances is in the middle of the road, as it gives him more scope for maneuvering should anything emerge from a side road. At the same time, should an accident occur, his position in the middle of the road might be regarded as contributory negligence.

If the automobilist is emerging from a side road into a main road he should bear in mind that the traffic on the main road has, so to speak, the right of way, and is justified in proceeding at a much faster pace than the traffic emerging from the side road; in fact, the onus, to a great extent, devolves on him to drive so as to cause the least possible risk of collision. If he is about to turn to the right there is little risk, because the traffic advancing to meet him will be either in the middle of the road or to its own right side, and, consequently, will leave him ample room. If, however, he is turning to the left, great caution should be observed, because, in this case, he will have to intercept the line of approaching traffic before he can get on to his proper side of the road. He should, consequently, slow down to a crawl and should hug the right side of the byroad until he is in the act of emerging on to the main road, when he should gradually curve to the left, keeping a careful lookout for approaching traffic.

If on so emerging he observes, for the first time, an automobile or other vehicle in very close proximity, his action must depend on circumstances, but should be absolutely instantaneous, and as such rapid decision can only be acquired by experience, the beginner cannot exercise too great caution. If there is time, of course, he should rush across to his own side of the road, letting the approaching vehicle pass behind him.

It may happen, however, that the driver of the approaching vehicle by an error of judgment swings over to his wrong side of the road in order to get in front of the emerging car. In such a case, the driver of the emerging car may turn sharp to the right into the center of the roadway and face in the same direction as the car on the main road, thus leaving it room to pass on either side of him. Of course, if the car emerges from the side road at such a very slow pace that it can be brought to a stop within three or four feet, and if a wide turn has been taken in the first instance, the best course would be to jam the brakes hard on.

If an accident does occur under any circumstances, whether

it is the fault of the automobilist or not, the driver should always pull up and give every assistance in his power. It would also be advisable for him at once to take the names and addresses of any witnesses, and interview them as to their view of the causes which led to the accident, taking careful note as to what they say. Should proceedings result, this evidence would prove invaluable.

Courtesy on the Road.

As regards road users other than automobilists, no consideration can be too great if automobile owners desire to earn the good will and favor of the general public. If a horse is restive, the autoist should pull up at once, and if necessary stop the engine. Should a horse, however, suddenly and unexpectedly begin to back across the road, and the driver is uncertain whether he can stop his car in time to prevent a collision, it is generally best to go for the opening and try to dash through before the way is blocked. There should be no hesitation, however. The automobilist should either jam his brakes on or accelerate. Cyclists should be given a wide berth, especially when the road surface is in a greasy condition, and the practice of keeping on the crown of the road, regardless of other people's convenience, should be avoided. In process of time all other road users will become accustomed to motor car traffic, and it will then be possible to drive far faster in safety and without causing inconvenience than it is in many places to-day.

Consideration for Tires.

The reliability and durability of tires depend mainly on the way in which the car is driven. Excessive wear is caused by letting in the clutch suddenly, by stopping abruptly, by taking corners fast, and by neglecting to steer clear of broken stones where possible. It is also advisable when patches of broken stones cannot be avoided to declutch momentarily while the hind wheels are passing over the patch.

SELF-TUITION IN DRIVING.

The following hints and tips constitute another effort to convey to the mind of the reader how he may teach himself to drive his own car, presuming that the vehicle is delivered to him at such time and place as make it impossible for him to obtain tuition at the hands of an expert familiar with the special make of car he has purchased. Such preliminary instruction is always to be recommended, but the consideration of time, cost and locality may render it out of the question. Let us presume the new car to be a light one of some 1,200 to 1,600 lbs., driven by a one or two-cylindered engine, through friction clutch, change speed gear, propeller-shaft and bevel gearing on differential gear of live axle. The power of the motor may be anything up to, say, 10 horsepower. We will also presume that the car has been delivered, and stands in the garage its owner has secured for it.

The Initial Trip.

For the first attempt, choose the most solitary stretch of road you know of. The novice does not require any sort of audience when learning to drive. We take it for granted that our novice is not ignorant of the dispositions of the car he has bought, that he has perused as much literature dealing directly with his purchase as he could conveniently come at, and that he knows, for instance, the difference between the water and gasolene tanks. This is knowledge he must possess, for no good purpose can be served by charging the wrong tank with the wrong fluid. This sounds particularly elementary, but the mistake has been made more than once, with decidedly exasperating results. Also, we take it that our novice has informed himself of the use and direction of movement of the controlling levers—that is to say, the direction in which to move the sparking lever in order to advance or retard the spark, the proper actuation of the accelerator lever, to let in or cut out the governor (if such be fitted), and of the air lever (if the supply is so controllable). We must also presume equal knowledge of the use of the gear changing and braking levers, and the clutch withdrawing and braking pedals. The car, of course, has been delivered with the electric wires all properly coupled up and the batteries charged. Here let us interpolate a little advice before proceeding further. Get these batteries recharged at the earliest opportunity. The first charge put into an accumulator does not last long, and the battery must not be expected to be on its best behavior until it has been recharged twice or thrice.

Charging Tanks.

Before the car is moved out of its garage the water tank should be filled with rainwater, if that is obtainable; if not, with the softest water than may be at hand. It is well to pour the water into the tank through a funnel fitted with a rather coarse strainer, as foreign bodies accidentally introduced into the water-cooling system cannot be withdrawn easily, and may do mischief. If your water system is provided with a drain-cock, open it before beginning to pour, and pour in for a little while it is running. This will prevent air-locks in the water system. Turn off the drain-cock—which, by the way, if present, should be found at the lowest point of the water system, when the jet has run solid—without spluttering or bubbling, and continue your filling until the level of the waste pipe from tank is reached, and the water trickles therefrom. Screw on cap of water tank. Now fill the gasolene tank. Among the accessories which should be supplied with the car will be found a funnel fitted with a gauze strainer. This must *always* be used when replenishing the gasolene tank, for dirt or other foreign matter introduced thereto will sooner or later give serious trouble, either by choking the gasolene supply pipe itself or choking up the spraying jet in the carbureter. It must be presumed that the lubricating tank is full, that grease boxes have been filled, and crank chamber, gear-box and differential gear case are properly supplied with the requisite quantities of oil. These are points which are often forgotten.

Starting the Engine.

Push your car out of its garage by hand, and then prepare to start your engine. Now, it is well to commence to perform the movements of levers, etc., necessary to this operation as they should in future be done, and, although this sequence of acts must vary in different makes of cars, we give them here as they are usually performed on a typical 10-horsepower car. The first thing to do—and be certain that you do it—is to make sure that your gear lever is in the free gear notch; to put on your side brakes, thus pulling out your clutch; to retard the spark almost to the lowest limit; and to get into the habit of doing these three things with certainty before you do anything else. Operation number 2. Move accelerator, or mixture lever, to the point which will give the easiest starting. In a typical car the accelerator lever is moved to a position about one-fourth down the rack segment, but with extra air admission most engines start with all or nearly all the air shut off at first. Operation 3. Open gasolene cock in gasolene supply pipe, allowing gasolene to flow to carbureter. If. lever control to air supply is fitted, place that lever in best position for starting. Also, if your engine has been standing some time and is cold, it is well to turn the starting handle two or three revolutions, which will expel all common atmosphere from the tubes, combustion chambers and valve boxes. Operation 4. Switch on current and turn on cylinder lubricators. Operation 5. Press the stud in the top of float feed chamber of carbureter, so as more or less to flood your carbureter with gasolene. Operation 6. Press starting handle in until it engages properly with the engine-shaft, and turn round slowly until you begin to feel the compression. The handle should always be turned against the compression by a pull towards the starter—never the reverse—as then, should the engine back fire, the handle will only be torn from the grasp and no harm be done. On the other hand, if the compression is pushed against, and a back fire takes place, the starter is sure to receive a nasty jar, if nothing more serious. So pull against your compression smartly and sharply, and the engine should start.

Ascertaining the Correct Mixture.

The next duty is to take steps to see that the engine is running to the best advantage. We must presume the reader knows which way to move the ignition lever to advance or retard the spark, and the necessary movement of the air lever to give more or less air; also how to actuate the accelerator lever or pedal, if you have got either or both. Advance the ignition until the engine begins to race. Then play a bit with the air lever, if you have one, or the ring cap opening and closing air ports to the carbureter, until your ear tells you that the engine is getting the mixture it likes best. If your ear does not inform you of this at once, you will very soon discover its proper note, which signifies that the engine is quite satisfied with the quality of the mixture you are feeding to it.

In the Driver's Seat.

If your circulating pump is friction-driven off the flywheel, as many pumps are, look at it and see that it is running properly. Assuming you have no pressure gauge, press any rubber connection in the water-circulating system between pump and cylinders to test by the pulsations there whether your pump is delivering properly or not. Now have a look at your cylinder lubricators, and see if they are feeding properly. The maker's catalogue should tell you how many drops a minute should be served; few catalogues do, but all should. With the car upon which these necessarily voluminous instructions are based, each drip should feed not less than five to seven drops per minute. It is usually easier to take your seat from the left than to squeeze in past the levers. Now sit down well and squarely before the wheel. Before you touch your side brakes lever, put your left foot on the clutch pedal, and depress it.

Manipulating the Control.

Now the clutch is withdrawn from driving contact with the flywheel, and cannot return thereto until you raise your foot.

So keep the pedal pressed down and take your side brakes off. See that the lever is right back. Now move the gear striking lever forward, so that the V-piece, or the trigger, whichever it may be fitted with, slips into the first speed slot or groove made to take it on the sector. Should the engine slow audibly, and grunt and snort more or less when moving the car away on the first speed, it is not running fast enough, and must be accelerated. Just how much you will soon find out. Now raise your foot gently—very gently— and easily until the car begins to draw away. An automobile should move away from rest just as the expert engine driver loves to take his flier away from a depot platform—that is, so that his passengers shall not be able to say when the train first moved. Keep your own side of the road, but not too close in. Now feel the steering, swing the car slightly from side to side, and learn how much lock a proportionate move-ment of the steering wheel controls.

Changing Gear.

Take a few corners on first speed. They will teach you just how much it is necessary to move your wheel to nego-tiate them.

Now to try a change of speed: With a governed engine, it is not necessary to touch the ignition or throttle or accelerator levers. Seize the handle portion of the gear-striking lever, and squeeze in the trigger lifter, if the lever is so fitted. Now press the pedal clutch right down to withdraw the clutch, and take the driving force off the car. With clutch so held out, move your gear lever forward until the trigger is past the first speed notch. Now release the trigger lifter, which you have hitherto been holding close to the handle of the gear lever, and let the trigger drop on to the smooth surface of the sector. Now slide the lever forward until you feel the trigger drop into the second speed notch, release lever, and raise your clutch pedal so as to let the clutch in gently. If a jarring noise is heard, it means that, instead of letting your trigger fall into the second speed notch before you let in your clutch, you slightly reversed the operation, with the result that the teeth of the driven toothed wheel of the second gear were trying to dodge into the spaces between the teeth of the driving toothed wheel when the latter was going the faster, and spoiling their nicely tooled entering edges in the attempt. Try changing again several times until the gears can be engaged without a lot of noise.

On the Top Speed.

Now you are on your second speed, and you had better keep on it awhile. Try some more corners, and get accustomed to the control of the car on the second speed. Press down the clutch pedal gently from time to time in order to realize just how much declutching will slow the car; but be careful to let it in gently as before. Do not let the car slow down too much, as picking up again on the second speed is not good for the gear. Press down your brake pedal from time to time, and learn how much stopping power it provides. When you feel quite comfortable on second speed, and realize that you have control of the car, change on to third, but select a fairly good length of straight road to run on this gear. The change is effected exactly as above described; that is, press down clutch pedal, move your lever forward into the next notch, and when it is there, let your pedal come up gently.

In practising changing speed, it is well to select a stretch of down grade, not a hill, but just a very slight slope, as then the car will run on, and you may be more deliberate about your pedal and lever movements. Unclutch frequently as before, and use the pedal brake gently to acquire a knowledge of the effect on third speed. Practise this well, for by judicious use of the clutch and gentle applications of the foot brake, it is frequently possible to slow up just enough to get through traffic without changing down. There is one further instruction to be remembered, and that is, when you have changed on to your third or top speed, you should retard or throttle down the engine speed, for it is not wise for the novice to drive at the height of his top speed right off the reel. You can accelerate the car gradually as you gain more confidence. The right thing to do is never to go fast till you perform every act of control automatically.

Attacking a Hill.

We must presume now that you have driven about on level roads until you can steer fairly well. The next thing to acquire is the knack of changing speed uphill in conformity with the gradient attacked. This, indeed, can hardly be called a knack—it is almost an instinct. First, wherever possible, it is well to put your car at a hill at its best gait on its top speed. It will rush up well at first, but gradually you will feel it slackening. You have your throttle wide open or your accelerator down already, and the only thing to be done in case the car will complete the climb on its top is to back down the ignition. Mind and do this, or the engine will knock—indeed, too early firing with the engine running slow has been known to break crankshafts. So back down as the car slows.

Presently it becomes apparent that it is not going over the hill on its top and the throb of the engine becomes accentuated. This is the moment—or, indeed, rather before, but you will learn it as you go—the psychological moment, to change down on to your second speed. Changing down is not so easy as changing up, and requires more practice. When properly done, grinding or groaning should in no way be in evidence, and there should be no forward or backward jerk of the car. It should glide on as though nothing had happened, and you alone in the car should be conscious that any change had been made. But, as we say, it is an instinct that comes by practice—sooner with some, later with more, and never with a few.

Withdrawing the Clutch.

There is one point, however, in changing down which may probably be observed. It is not necessary to withdraw the clutch wholly—indeed, some well-known drivers say that, if the change is effected at the proper moment, there is no need to withdraw the clutch at all; but we do not advise the novice to try. The clutch should be withdrawn sufficiently to admit of it slipping, just how much varies with every car, and the knowledge thereof will only come with practice. Do not delay until the last moment for changing down to a lower gear, but drive upon that gear upon which you are running to the best possible advantage. Keep the engine running at its normal speed as long as possible by the manipulation of the throttle and sparking advance lever. When the speed of the engine begins to drop slightly change at once.

Gentle Handling.

In getting over the top of a hill, do not be in too great a hurry to change up again. The man who bangs in his second or his third before the engine is ready to take the car up shortens the life of his vehicle, besides laying up a store of trouble for himself. The true automobilist will come to feel for his car, and to learn just exactly what it likes and how it likes it. If you breast the brow of the hill on your first, wait until you hear your engine race before you change on to your second, and then wait again similarly before you slip in third. In pulling up, use your brakes gently. There are times, of course, when the brakes must be used for a sudden stop; but for all ordinary slacks, the throttle should be closed or the clutch pedal should be depressed and the car allowed to slow down naturally and easily.

Coasting Slopes.

Given average intelligence, the novice will find that a couple of hours' practice will be sufficient to permit him to manage his machine upon the open roads with safety to other people. Whenever the car will coast, at a reasonable speed without the engine driving, the driver will find that this is the safest, quietest, and most economical way of descending slopes. With the 10 horse-power machine, upon which these driving hints have been formed particularly, it has only been found necessary to press down the clutch pedal and withdraw clutch from contact with the flywheel, letting the clutch in gently as the bottom of the slope is approached, so that the engine might take up the drive.

Picking up the Drive.

Just which speed should be attained before the clutch is let in will depend precisely upon what grade is next to be attacked; but if the descent continues gently or is followed by a level stretch, then the third or top speed should be engaged. The car gaining some momentum from the descent, the engine will be found to pick the drive up very nicely. If, however, the drop down is followed almost immediately by a rise, then the clutch should be let in and the gear engaged earlier, in order that a good rush may be made at the opposite slope. When you have learnt your car a bit, and feel fairly sure of yourself, it is well to accelerate the engine more or less for this sprint.

Throttling Down the Free Engine.

In descending hills with the engine free, it should be throttled right down, so as to cause it to run as slowly as possible, the ignition being well backed at the same time. Before striking a gear and letting in the clutch, the driver must not omit to open his throttle, advance spark, and get the engine running at a speed sufficient to take up the drive as soon as the clutch is let in. When a switch is placed ready to hand, the current may be cut off altogether, so that the engine stops, if the character and length of the descent will warrant this, so that when the moment comes for taking up the drive, the clutch let in, the current switched on, and throttle opened, the momentum of the car will restart the engine. The precise speed and grade on which one's engine can be started in this way is only to be known by practice, so that when our novice has acquired some skill and confidence he should essay to seek the same.

Driving on the Reverse.

Driving backward must be essayed carefully, and thought must be taken to press the clutch well out before moving the gear-striking lever from the free to the reversing notch on the quadrant. It, of course, will be recognized that we are discussing a car on which all the speed-changing is performed by the movement of one lever. When an auxiliary lever has to be actuated to strike the reversing gear, then care must be taken to leave the forward striking gear lever in the free notch on the quadrant before the reversing lever is touched. With the clutch pedal pressed well down, move the lever to the reverse notch, and, keeping your foot firmly upon the pedal, turn partially round to the right in your seat, so that you can look square out of the back of your car over the center or side. In this wise, you will find it much easier to handle and steer your vehicle to a nicety when running astern than if you merely turn your head and look over your shoulder. Now let your clutch in gently, and as the car begins to go astern ascertain just the amount of helm it is necessary to give it for any desired movement. As your body is turned to the right, you have only your left hand for the wheel, but this will not be found difficult after a few trials.

The novice is strongly advised to select a wide and deserted stretch of road, and to practise reversing and steering backward until he has fairly got the hang of the effect of his lock when going backward. When you have traveled back to the desired position, do not fail to declutch, and if you are going to stop move your gear lever to the free notch, or take your reversing gear out with your reversing lever if your car is so fitted.

Entering the Garage.

Driving in and out of the garage or barn may give the novice some concern, and in this connection we would urge strongly that neither in coming out nor going in to such shelter should the beginner proceed on any other but his first speed. It is because cars have so frequently to be backed out of their shelters that we have already urged the novice to practise steering backward. Whether he will go into his garage backward and thus leave his vehicle in position to come straight out, or the reverse, must depend altogether upon circumstances; but if there should be a drop into the stable of sufficient gradient to allow the car to run down by its own weight, we should advise him to drop in gently backward, with clutch out and foot on brake pedal, for it is less troublesome so to steer the car than to drive out backward up a slope.

After the Drive.

Now, when the drive is over and the car is to be put away, the man who wishes to keep all things in order and ready for an immediate start will devote a little time to replenishing with lubricating oil and kerosene. As soon as the engine is stopped, and the car is housed, lift the motor bonnet, and with your kerosene oilcan give the pistons two or three good squirts of kerosene through the cocks in the combustion chambers provided for the purpose. If your engine is innocent of these fittings, unscrew your sparking plugs and dose through the ports. Some people will tell you to use gasolene, but most prefer good kerosene. The effect of gasolene in loosening the piston rings vanishes in a very short time, and if your car remains unused for a day or two, the engine will not turn so easily when you come to start it up. Before turning off your compression cocks, or replacing your sparking plugs, turn the engine round several times by hand. This will cause the kerosene to cleanse the cylinder walls and rings. Fill up lubricators if they require it, and charge gasolene and water tanks, being careful afterward to screw down cap and vent screw on the former tightly.

Do not leave your switch on. If you do, you may find your battery run down when you next desire to drive.

If you have time at your disposal, it is well to make a careful survey of your car, and to see that no nuts have worked loose and that no bearing has run hot. Further, if you have any respect for your paint and upholstery, get a covering sheet of canvas and cover up your automobile before leaving it. Keep it covered always when standing in the garage.

Negotiating Road Risks.

When driving, always bear in mind that in the common

state of judicial and public opinion no excuse of any sort will serve you if you are damaged or cause damage by passing on your wrong side. To do so when a lumbering dray occupies the crown of the highway and your proper section of the road is blocked while there is ample room elsewhere is at times a great temptation, and we do not say that it may not occasionally be taken advantage of. But always bear in mind that the risk of vehicles closing in, of children of younger and of older growth darting out in front of you, is yours and yours alone. If you are one jot or tittle in the wrong, no matter how selfish or stupid those whose property or persons you may injure, you will have little or no consideration when called upon to pay the piper.

When overtaking traffic and finding by the time you arrive abreast of the vehicle you intend to pass that another coming in the opposite direction will be there before you, you should so speed your car that when the road is clear you will be able to go ahead without changing speed or using your brakes. If, however, you are on your top speed and your car has slowed down so that your engine is thumping, change down before you attempt to pass the vehicle in front.

Do your best to accommodate your speed to the traffic you are negotiating, so as to change speed and use your brakes as seldom as possible. By attention to this you will soon find your eye becoming educated to distances and speeds and you will be astonished to find how nicely these can be timed to drive with the least possible trouble.

ANOTHER LESSON IN DRIVING.

The methods that are recommended for learning to drive a motor car are almost as numerous as the makes of successful automobiles, and, in order that all the important points may be touched upon and nothing overlooked, still another set of instructions for new owners and drivers, from the standpoint of an automobilist of experience and authority, is appended:

Learning the Steering and Control.

A new owner will do well in the first place to study the construction and working of his car, as far as possible, while it is stationary. As part of this course, he should spend some time in the driver's seat, and accustom himself to the positions of the steering wheel and the various levers. Then he may venture out on the road in the company of an experienced driver, and by first resting his right hand lightly on the steering wheel, learn the effect of the different movements of the wheel on the course taken by the car. Gradually he will be able to take charge of the steering entirely from the left-hand seat, and then, occupying the driver's seat, may learn to steer the car on its first speed.

We will now suppose that you are able to steer the car, and have a general acquaintance with its various features, but otherwise are very much left to your own resources. Naturally, you are anxious to go for a drive; and here we may give a hint as to the route to be pursued on this occasion. Let it be a circular tour of short radius, and with home as center. In this way the risk of an expensive return in case of a breakdown is greatly reduced, and you will have the advantage, in all probability, of being well acquainted with the whole of the road traversed.

Preliminary Attentions.

Before starting out, the various nuts and bolts should be looked over, especially on a new car, and the brakes and steering gear connections should receive particular attention. The quantity of gasolene in the tank should be ascertained. If no gauge glass is fitted, a celluloid or glass tube may be inserted, a finger placed on the top, and the tube lifted out. The height of the gasolene in the tube will indicate the quantity in the tank. Or a clean white stick or paper spill will serve as a guide by discoloring the portion moistened. If more gasolene is required, it should be poured in through a funnel having a fine wire gauze strainer. This strainer should be supplemented by a piece of fine white cambric, as this, when saturated with gasolene, resists the passage of any water that may happen to be in the can. Any water collecting in the cambric should be thrown away. See that the spout of the funnel is clean outside and in. A little gasolene or kerosene should be injected into each cylinder to free the piston rings and (in the case of the gasolene) to facilitate the obtaining of the first explosion. The lubricators should be turned on, and the caps of the grease cup given a turn—in fact, the car should be lubricated throughout.

After having seen that the gear lever is in the out-of-gear position, the carbureter should receive attention. It may be emptied of any stale gasolene it may contain. The mixture regulator may be set to cut down the quantity of air; and, the gasolene cock having been turned on, the float may be agitated so as to flood the carbureter. The throttle valve should be opened. The electric current should be switched on; and be careful to see that the timing lever is set well back. The next thing to do is to release the compression, if means for so doing are provided, but this is only usually necessary with large engines.

Starting the Engine.

The starting handle should be turned round clockwise (in most cars) until the resistance of the compression is felt. If this occurs as the handle is going downward, turn the handle back half a turn or so, and then try again until the compression is felt as the handle is beginning to come upward. The handle should be held with the fingers of the right hand under it, and the thumb not over it. When the compression is felt, give a strong and continuing pull upward, when, if all is in order, the motor will start. If the ignition were too far advanced, the explosion would drive the handle backward; and if you were pushing the handle down at the time, the chances are your wrist would be broken or so severely sprained as to be useless for some time to come. But if you are pulling up, the back fire simply unbends the fingers; and though you may be a bit scared, you are not likely to be hurt.

If the motor will not start after a few attempts, the ignition may be slightly advanced, and different mixtures may be tried for the gas. If this will not do, try further injections of gasolene into the cylinders. Test the ignition to see that it is sparking properly. Sometimes it will be found that the valves having become dirty do not move freely; and if they remain open when they ought to close, the engine cannot work.

As soon as the engine starts, the ignition may be advanced somewhat, and the throttle partly closed. Your passengers having got aboard, you are ready to start. Hold the clutch out by the foot, and move the change gear lever into the first speed notch. If it will not enter easily, allow the clutch to engage slightly for a moment, and then try to get in gear again. As soon as the gear is engaged, the clutch should be let in very gradually, the throttle being opened to provide plenty of power. As the clutch engages, the car will move off, and the run will be begun. In starting, changing speed, etc., the finger catch (if any) must be grasped with the handle of the lever, but the catch should be released when it is clear of its notch, so that it may be ready to drop into the fresh notch as soon as the lever brings it opposite thereto.

Sometimes when the motor will not consent to start in the ordinary way, it may be prevailed upon to do its duty by letting in the first speed and clutch, and pushing the car. Of course, the driver must be in position so that he can steer the car and control it directly the motor begins to function.

Changing Speed.

After the car has got into its stride on its first speed, the gear may be raised to the next speed. To effect this, the sparking should be advanced so as to hustle up the motor, the clutch taken well out, and the gear lever moved, with as much decision and promptitude as possible, into the next higher notch. The clutch is let in again quickly, but gradually, and the whole operation should be performed with address, so that the speed of the car may not be sensibly diminished during the operation. Never put in a higher gear until you have become perfectly acquainted with the next lower one. It is very tempting to see how fast the car can go, or how fast you dare let it go, but the temptation should be sternly resisted during your novitiate, otherwise you may never become an expert. After the car has fairly started, the mixture may be varied slightly until the best adjustment has been obtained; it should then be set with a little more air. The throttle, too, should be opened only so far as will allow of the car being driven at the desired speed with the ignition well advanced.

On reaching a hill, the speed of the car should be kept up at first by opening the throttle further and further as required. When the limit of this adjustment has been reached, the ignition should be gradually retarded, especially if the engine sets up a knocking noise. Some drivers are very skilful at coaxing cars uphill without lowering the gear, but this practice is not to be commended. If the engine begins to labor or the speed of the car has fallen to that of the next lower gear, that gear should be brought into operation. The motor should not be allowed to run too fast during the change; and the change should be effected quickly, as the speed of the car will fall very rapidly while the motive power is cut off. The directions for changing speed are soon given, but the amount of success with which the driver carries them out depends upon practice and skill.

Coasting, Braking, and Reversing.

Down grades will call for different treatment of the engine, according to their steepness and length. If the hill is only a short one, the engine may be left running at a slow speed and the clutch disengaged. If the hill is a long one, the motor may be stopped altogether, and the car allowed to run down by gravity; the quiet running will be found a welcome change. On nearing the bottom of a hill, the clutch should be gradually let in so as to start up the motor again. If the hill is very steep, the car should be kept well in hand from the very top. The first (lowest) speed should be put in and the current switched off; thus the engine will be converted into a pump, and will serve as an auxiliary brake, though this is not possible, of course, where the application of the pedal brake throws out the clutch.

Both the foot and the hand brakes should be tested soon after starting out on a run. If the car shows a disposition to get away down a hill, the clutch should be let in gently with the ignition switched off or the throttle quite closed. This will serve to limit the speed of the car. Broadly speaking, and in a general way, the brakes should be applied as little as possible. One sometimes sees a car come dashing up to its destination, and pull up in a few yards. This only shows that the driver has more control over the machine than he has over himself. It is smart, no doubt, especially for the tires.

Nothing is gained, but rather the contrary, by applying the brakes so hard as to skid the wheels. It is really much more clever to throttle down gradually and let the car arrive at the desired point upon momentum only.

On reaching one's destination, the current should be switched off, the gasolene tap closed, and the dripping of the lubricators stopped. The first and the last of these operations should be performed on stops of even short duration.

If it is desired to reverse the car, it must first be brought to a dead stop, the engine of course being left running, and the clutch disengaged. The reverse gear is now put in, and the clutch very gradually re-engaged. It is as well to practise reversing in a wide space at first, as the steering will be found somewhat awkward. Remember that if you encounter a hill that your car cannot climb, even on the first speed, it may be able to get up on the reverse, being driven backward, of course, for the purpose.

As a general rule, do not advance either the timing of the sparking or the opening of the throttle suddenly. The changes effected by these means should always be made gradually. And, finally, practise with your car until the control of it becomes perfectly automatic. Until then you can never trust yourself to do the right thing in an emergency.

Sources of Side-slip.

One of the worst evils the driver has to contend with is that of side-slip, and it is not to be surprised at if he loses his head somewhat on the first two or three occasions that this diversion occurs. The accident is nearly always compound—that is to say, the slipping in itself is not dangerous; but if the car strikes anything else, that thing will be damaged as well as the car.

It is a well-known fact in mechanics that if a sliding movement occurs between two contacting bodies, the one that is in motion may be moved at an angle to its path with comparative ease. In driving, therefore, on slippery surfaces, great care should be taken to avoid any variation from the true rolling motion of the wheels on the road. The variation may occur in several ways. For instance, if the engine be suddenly accelerated, the driving wheels will tend to spin round instead of merely rolling forward. Again, if the brakes be suddenly applied, the road wheels may rotate slower than the progress of the car corresponds to, and, indeed, they may cease to rotate at all, merely sliding along. Further, in passing over an uneven road the car may bounce, so that the wheels at times are actually out of contact with the road surface. Under any of these conditions, a very slight disturbing force will be enough to deflect the car from its straight course, and cause side-slip.

So long as the road is hard and dry, the friction between the tires and the road surface will be ample to prevent skidding; but if the hard smooth surface be covered with thin mud, or if a comparatively soft surface be covered with thick mud, the car will be prevented from obtaining a firm grip and may begin to slide at any moment. The same thing may, or will, happen on roads that are deep in dust; but the worst surface is undoubtedly ice that has begun to thaw.

Another source of side-slip is found in connection with street car lines. The lines themselves, or the tracks in which they are laid, often project above the general level of the road, or sometimes are depressed below the same, in either case forming ridges which tend to prevent the car traveling at an angle thereto. The disturbing effect is greatest when the lines are wet. Probably the fact that cars are driven from the back and steered by the front contributes to their tendency to slip, as the rear part has a disposition to push round the front, on one side or the other. Of course, the greatest tendency to side-slip occurs when the car is being driven round a corner, as the centrifugal force then exerts a considerable lateral pressure upon the vehicle.

To Avoid Skidding.

To avoid side-slip our novice may take certain precautions. We will not say, do not take the car out when the roads are slippery, because it may not always be possible to follow that advice; and further, though the roads may be perfectly safe as a rule, you may find that a sprinkling cart has made them quite the reverse over more or less restricted sections. But when a greasy stretch is encountered, proceed slowly, especially in making turns. If the car begins to slip, keep your wits about you and begin to steer in the direction of the slip. This may be exactly contrary to your inclination, but it will tend to restore the grip of the wheels on the road; and as soon as this result is attained, you may begin carefully to steer again in the direction you wish to follow. As the camber or transverse curve of the road surface helps to promote side-slip, one should drive as much on the crown of the road as consideration for other traffic will allow.

In turning corners to the right, take the right side of the road; but in turning corners to the left, only take the left side of the road if you can see that the course is clear. If you keep on the inside of the corner, the transverse inclination of the road will help to get the car round. In taking corners, it is a good plan to declutch, and also to abstain from putting on the brakes; the chances of getting round safely are much increased if the car simply rolls round the curve. Street car tracks should be crossed at as nearly a right angle as possible. But if you are running along a crowded road laid with car tracks, and wish to get on to or off from the track, the steering should be as gradual as possible, so that if the wheels refuse to take the ridges, the disturbing effect will be very small. One grain of comfort we can give: Side-slip is practically never accompanied by overturning, unless the car catches against some low object.

Non-slip Devices.

Prevention, however, is better than cure, and it is well to adopt some form of non-slipping device. Nearly all of these devices consist of some apparatus fitted to the tires and designed to cut through the grease, and so obtain a hold on the firm surface below.

A fairly effective non-slipper may be improvised by winding strong cord round the tire and felloes in spiral form. The ends of the cord must be carefully secured, and the cord itself examined frequently, and renewed as required. In any case it is best to fit all four wheels with the non-slippers.

Choice of Track.

Too many drivers simply take the road as it comes without troubling to select the best path. Possibly they are not aware that every bump means waste of power and increased wear to the car. But such is undoubtedly the case. One can often detect the fact that the driver is an experienced cyclist from the way in which he picks his course. We do not mean, of course, that the driver should keep the car perpetually on the wriggle, but simply that where he has the choice to make, he should take the line which will be best for the vehicle and most comfortable for the passengers. Thus a smooth surface is to be preferred to a rough one; dry ground is better than wet; the crown of the road gives better running than the sloping sides; and all reasonable care should be taken to avoid holes and loose stones. If a patch of new macadam cannot be avoided, it is best to drive up to it at a good speed and then declutch, so that the wheels merely roll over the stones, without being subjected to the additional strain set up by driving. If the momentum is not sufficient to carry the car the full length of the patch, the remainder should be driven over quietly at slow speed.

Emergencies and General Conduct.

As a rule, the steering of the car, like the manipulation of the throttle and spark timing, should be performed gradually. It is very bad for the tires and most provocative of side-slip, to swing the steering wheel suddenly from one position to another. Perhaps the only times when this may be excused is when accidents would otherwise occur; as, for instance, when people, especially children, rush across in front of one without looking. Again, if a car begins to run back down a hill, the steering wheel should be promptly rotated so as to change the course of the car to a transverse direction. The brakes should be applied at the same time to prevent, if possible, charging into the bank, fence or other side of the road. It is much better to collide with the fence at the top of the hill than at the bottom—we mean, stop the car before it has gathered speed.

The automobilist's reputation being in many places none of the best, it is most important to drive as inoffensively as possible. It is not enough merely to have regard to the safety of other road users. One must avoid driving in such a way as to let them think that they have been in danger. It is almost, if not quite, as bad to offend a man's dignity by running him fine (as he imagines) as to knock him down. As a general rule, it is far safer to pass behind people than in front of them, when their path intersects your own. The horn or gong should be used fairly freely, though in blasts of short duration, the idea being rather to comply with the law than directly to profit by the signaling.

Never drive so fast that you cannot come to a dead stop within the length of road for the time being seen to be clear. Do not discommode or endanger other users of the road or the inhabitants of roadside houses by raising an excessive amount of dust, and do not bespatter pedestrians with mud. These things may seem a good deal to ask, but are not too much, we

think, to require from one who is after all merely taking his
pleasure in public.

Speed Limits.

Speed limits are misguiding. There can be no harm morally
in disregarding them where the road and its approaches can
be seen to be clear; and they do not license one to travel up
to them, where to do so would be to endanger the public. With
the best intentions in the world, one is liable to travel too
fast unwittingly at times. Thus, after a clear run at a good
speed in the open, the pace is reduced to what seems a mere
crawl on reaching a village. The driver contrasts his crawl
with the speed he has just been running at; the village resi-
dent, on the contrary, compares it with the rate of progress of
the local horses—and the resulting impressions are naturally
somewhat different. A speedometer has its uses.

Do not confine your attention to the road merely; have an
eye open for somnambulistic pedestrians with a weakness for
leaving one path for the other with no regard for the traffic
on the roadway. Treat them gently; it spoils their temper
to wake them suddenly. Do not be satisfied with being in the
right; keep out of scrimmages at all costs, for the automobilist
cannot reckon on justice in these days. Observe the rules of
the road, that is, keep to the right when meeting other vehicles,
and to the left when overtaking them. But these rules must
be disobeyed if necessary to avoid an accident.

Driving through City Traffic.

In driving through towns and cities one should be careful
to see that the course is clear before attempting to overtake
vehicles in front. It is not always necessary to swing round
to the off side in order to ascertain the possibility of getting
by, as many vehicles can be seen right through from end to
end. When about to turn off to the right or left, in crowded
thoroughfares, it is a good rule that the driver should hold
out one hand to that side; and for stopping he should hold
one hand straight up. As you approach a cross street, the windows you see in that street often reflect what is coming up to

your road; and by looking at the windows at your side, you can also often see reflected the traffic that is coming behind you.

Pedestrians are allowed to walk where they like on a road provided they do not unreasonably obstruct other traffic. A led horse should be passed (in either direction) on the side of the man leading it; but this is convention rather than law. Street cars should be met and overtaken on the right side of the road.

Horses, Cattle, and Cyclists.

Horses are now fairly well accustomed to motor cars in most districts; but in remote places many owners have taken little or no trouble to educate their animals to the new method of locomotion, and special care must be exercised in dealing with them. In meeting a doubtful horse, it is best to proceed slowly and be ready to stop at any moment, whether the driver holds up his hand or not. Some horses have an unpleasant trick of looking perfectly unconcerned until almost up to the car, and then suddenly backing right across the road. Under these circumstances, the automobilist will have to act very promptly if a collision is to be avoided.

In overtaking nervous horses, it is best to drive quickly and quietly, so as to shorten the incident as much as possible. Unless time is precious, one may offer to spend a few minutes in improving a badly trained horse's acquaintance with motor cars. The horse owner's opinions on the subject are generally as much improved as those of his animal. Great care should be exercised in overtaking wagons carrying poles and other long burdens; as, if the driver draws his horse over to one side, the tail of the load swings across the road, and momentarily obstructs the other side.

The perfect control one has over a car tempts one to assume that all other road users are in equal command of their means of conveyance. But this is a very unsafe assumption. Every rider and driver has a period of inexperience; and even those who have got over their novitiate are liable to lose their heads at times, as, for example, on hearing a car coming up behind them. The only safe course, therefore, is to see how much, not how little, space one can give cyclists, horsemen, and others. Remember especially that a cyclist's position is always more or less dangerous when the road is wet and slopes to the gutters.

PART V.

DIFFICULTY IN STARTING.

In the pages immediately following we point out the remedies for most of the ordinary troubles met with by the motorist from time to time, beginning with those which may cause difficulty in starting. No beginner should be discouraged, however, at the length of the list of possible causes of trouble. He would be indeed an unlucky driver that experienced repeated difficulties in starting and the list given is that of possible, not probable, causes of annoyance and delay. It will arm the motorist against what may happen.

Difficulty in Starting—It has been truly said that a gasolene motor is a thing of freak notions; it has been known to be running perfectly all one day and almost impossible to start the next morning, notwithstanding the fact that not a single piece of the mechanism has been disturbed—by mortal hand. Yet, where a motor stops or fails to start, let it be known there is a cause; the chief difficulty for the beginner—and sometimes for the wisest expert—is to locate the cause, which, once discovered, is usually easily remedied. Trouble in starting, except in cold weather, when atmospheric conditions determine things, is usually traceable to some minor disarrangement and probably 90 per cent of all such troubles may safely be traced either to the ignition system or the carbureter and its very close relatives. Aside from the reasons here given for a motor failing to start as the operator would have it, there have been other reasons and there will in the future be found still more. Ordinarily the operator who has difficulty in starting his motor will find the reason set forth in the paragraphs under this heading; if the reason is still remote the case will probably be a difficult one and beyond the imagination of any man who is any distance from the balky piece of machinery. Difficulties in starting are taken up in their probable order of likelihood.

Ignition.

Batteries Weak—Test each dry cell with an ammeter; if it shows under 5 or 6 ampères, replace it with a new one. Better still, discard the set and put in a new one. If there are two sets and each set is weak, connect the two sets in series which will suffice for a time. It is well to always carry an ammeter so that in purchasing new cells they may be tested New ones should test in the neighborhood of from 15 to 17 ampères.

Storage batteries must not be tested with an ammeter or a voltmeter. Attach a wire to one pole and snap the free end across the other pole. If a large, snappy spark results, the battery is all right. A storage battery never should be permitted to be completely exhausted; nor should it be permitted to stand without some use for any length of time, otherwise it may be ruined.

Switch Off—A most common oversight, even with old motorists.

Loose Connections—Battery terminals or wire leading to switch or coil disconnected.—If switch is on and vibrators do not buzz, trace the wires for the disconnection.

Incorrect Wiring—This will not be the case where the motor has been running and no alterations have been made; it may occur when the wiring has been changed or replaced after overhauling. Consult the diagram of wiring as secured from the seller and see that the wiring scheme is correct.

Plugs—(a) Plugs fouled with oil or carbon—Remove and clean.

(b) Points on make-and-break sooted or fouled—Clean with fine file or emery paper.

(c) Short circuit through broken or cracked porcelain—Replace with new plug.

(d) Points too close or too far apart—Reset to have 1/32 inch gap.

Coil—(a) Vibrators stuck—Readjust after cleaning to remove possible pitting or dirt, destroying contact.

(b) Tension of vibrator spring too great for partially run-down batteries.—Readjust to meet battery condition.

(c) Coil wet—Remove and take to coil man for repairs.

(d) Condenser in coil punctured (through use of too high voltage, for instance)—Same remedy.

(e) Wire from battery or commutator disconnected—Replace.

(f) Secondary wire disconnected or broken (but this will not prevent vibrators from buzzing).

Spark Lever—(a) Connections slipped, retarding spark.—Reset as per information obtained when purchasing car.

(b) Connections from spark lever to commutator disconnected—Go over and secure as originally.

Carbureter—Gasolene.

(a) Throttle closed—Open.

(b) Gasolene tank empty—Fill.

(c) Shut-off valve in gasolene line closed—Open.

(d) Water in gasolene tank, carbureter or line—Drain from bottom of carbureter, or disconnect pipe at lowest point, if there is no drain cock, and let about a pint drain off.

In winter water will freeze in carbureter or pipe line and absolutely shut off the gasolene supply.

(e) Dirt in carbureter, choking spray nozzle—Drain carbureter and if necessary take out to clean, being careful not to disturb adjustments.

(f) Float level too high—This will cause flooding of carbureter, too rich mixture and sluggish starting, if any.

Inasmuch as carbureters differ, no rule for changing the float level can be laid down. See Carbureters.

(g) Float punctured or leaky, preventing valve from shutting off and causing carbureter to flood—Secure new float.

(h) Float level too low, causing weak mixture.

(i) Air valve spring tension too great, causing too rich mixture; too weak, causing motor to take too much air and too little gasolene.

Lack of Suction.

(a) Valves stuck, holding open, preventing suction and compression. This will occur in cold weather if the stems are gummed with oil.

(b) Valve springs weak or broken. If weak, stretch out for temporary repair; if broken, remove and place an iron washer over the stem and between the pieces of spring.

(c) Poor compression through fouled valves—Remove and grind. See "Useful Information."

(d) Leak in intake pipe joints—Set up cap screws, nuts or whatever holds pipe to cylinders; if necessary put in new packing of asbestos, with shellac on either side.

(e) Relief cocks open—Close.

(f) Plugs not tight—Screw in close, use copper gasket if plug has shoulder. If threads are worn use litharge and glycerine, in paste, to take up wear, same as plumber would use red lead.

(g) Valve pocket caps or valve cage ring nuts loose—Set down; use litharge and glycerine if badly worn.

(h) Piston rings stuck—Put kerosene in cylinders, leave stand few hours to loosen rings.

(i) Carbureter connection to intake pipe loose—Tighten and put in new gasket if necessary.

In Winter—Cold Engine.

(a) Flood carbureter.

(b) Close air intake with cloth,

(c)   Prime cylinders with half teaspoonful gasolene.

(d)   Advance spark little more than usual, because of lag in ignition.

(e)   Soak cloth with gasolene and put in air intake so gas can be drawn into cylinders.

(f)   Keep throttle well open.

(g)   Warm carbureter with cloth soaked in hot water; or pour hot water on carbureter, being sure no water gets into air intake.

Valves Set Wrong.

If the valves are set so as to open and close at the wrong time the motor will not start and will not run. Thus it is essential that the valve setting be known and known to be correct.

PART VI.

INVOLUNTARY STOPS.

Nothing is more annoying to the motorist than to have his car suddenly stop without apparent cause. Whether he be driving on city streets or touring the country roads such a stoppage may often be embarrassing in the extreme unless the driver is equipped with sufficient knowledge of possible causes to locate the trouble and apply the proper remedy. The most likely causes are indicated below and the respective remedies are duly prescribed.

Involuntary Stops—Of course, the car may pull up for defects other than those connected with the engine, but the most frequent causes of stoppages (with the exception of tire troubles) are due to failures of the motor. With a little experience one can often guess the cause of the trouble from the way in which the stoppages occur. Thus, if the firing cease suddenly, it is probably due to a breakage in the electric system, or to the seizing of one of the pistons, or to one of the valves sticking or breaking, or, lastly, to obstruction of the carbureter. On the other hand, if the engine expires gradually, the trouble probably arises from failure of the water circulation, or the supply of gasolene or lubricating oil, or to the choking of the gauzes in the carbureter by dust or ice, or to the leakage of the float or of the compression. Thirdly, if the firing is intermittent, it indicates a discharged battery, a loose electrical connection, or a cracked sparking plug. We do not mean to say that this analysis is exhaustive, but it is a guide which will generally be found correct.

Failure of Gasolene.

We will consider some of the defects to which the various elements of a car are subject. If the gasolene is fed from the tank by gravity, the supply may cease owing to the fact that air is unable to enter the tank. The remedy is to unscrew the cap and let more air in. The cap should have a small airhole in it. Some tanks are provided with two caps, one having an airhole and the other not. The former is used during running; and evaporation is prevented by using the latter at other times. If the gasolene be fed under pressure, failure of the pressure will, of course, cause failure of supply. The most common cause of failure of supply is that the stock is exhausted. This generally means negligence, and it is always a good plan to carry one or two spare cans of gasolene to be used in case of emergency.

Carbureter Complaints.

The carbureter's most usual complaint consists in stoppage of the jet by some solid particle carried into it by the gasolene. If this be suspected while the car is running, the air supply may be reduced suddenly, so as to cause increased suction at the jet. If this does not remove the obstacle, one should agitate the float. If the carbureter floods and overflows from the jet chamber, the trouble has probably been got over; if it does not, the passage to the jet should be opened, and a fine wire pushed through. Do not use a needle or other hard wire for this purpose, as it may break off in the jet. A piece of florist's wire, or wire off a mineral water bottle, if not too thick, will serve very well. If the carbureter is provided with a well or filter, this should be opened, so that the precipitate may be removed. The cock in the gasolene supply pipe should be turned off first, otherwise a quantity of gasolene will be wasted. Or it may be found that water has collected in the carbureter; this may be removed in the same way by emptying the well.

Float and Needle Defects.

A more awkward situation is created when the float leaks; this, of course, upsets the balance of the carbureter, and prevents the gasolene standing at the right height. One can easily tell if there is gasolene in the float by taking it out and shaking it. To cure the trouble, warm the float and apply a light to it; the gasolene will be vaporized, and will catch light at the hole by which it entered. Put out the flame, mark the hole, and, if it is not large enough to pour out the gasolene through, make another hole in the top of the float and pour it out through that. When the float is empty, re-solder both holes, using as little solder as possible, so as not to alter the weight of float. This method should only be resorted to in an emergency, however, as it might result in much more harm than good. Another way is simply to remove the float and regulate the supply to the jet by the cock in the feed-pipe.

A defective needle valve will upset the working of the carbureter. If it arise from bending of the needle, it may be remedied by straightening the needle, and, if necessary, regrinding-in the valve. This grinding operation is similar to that of grinding-in the motor valves, which should be studied. Sometimes the gauze screens through which the air and gasolene are admitted get so clogged up with dirt that the supply of these two fluids becomes insufficient. A little careful cleaning is all that is required. In cold, damp weather a block of ice will sometimes form on the gauze screen at the carbureter end of the inlet pipe, and the simplest way to deal with this is to remove the screen. Many carbureters are provided with heating arrangements, and if these are fitted with a cock, the cock should be opened on such occasions.

Ignition Troubles.

The ignition is a most fruitful source of stoppages, especially when on the battery and coil system; and the spark gap device, if not of much use as an intensifier, is certainly of considerable value as an index of the state of the system. If a good spark is shown at the gap one may fairly conclude that the ignition is in fair order up to that point, and first attention may therefore be given to the sparking plug. If there is no spark gap, one may detach the high-tension wire from the plug and hold the end about a quarter of an inch from any metallic part of the engine. Hold the wire by the insulation, and, better still, wrap a thick cloth round this; then turn the starting handle, and see whether a good spark passes from the end of the wire. If it does, unscrew the plug from the cylinder, and probably you will find that the points, and very likely the end of the porcelain also, are covered with a carbon deposit. Clean this off with gasolene and an old toothbrush, and polish up the faces of the points with fine emery cloth. See that the points are· in line, and about a millimeter (or 1/25 in. to 1/26 in.) apart; some recommend 1/32 inch. Examine the porcelain to see that it is not broken, cracked, or loose. Also make sure that the central wire is properly secured; if it can twist round, the spark points may get out of line when the high-tension wire is attached, and then, of course, they will be too far apart for the spark to jump. The porcelain may be tightened by carefully screwing in the gland nut.

Now reconnect the wire to the plug, and lay the plug on the motor, so that only the metal body thereof is in contact with it. Turn the starting handle again, and see whether a good spark occurs at the points of the plug; if it does not, try another plug. Do not forget to switch the current on while testing. It should be remembered that water is a good conductor, and that if the exposed part of the porcelain is wet, the current will pass through it instead of across the points. Drying the porcelain will suffice in this case.

It may be, however, that no spark passes from the end of the high-tension wire, or that, though a spark is obtained, it will not continue for any length of time; and the test should always be continued for, say five or ten seconds. If the sparking gets weaker and perhaps expires during this time, it shows that the battery is run down, and such current as it gives is only due to temporary recuperation. This should be remembered when testing the high-tension wire or the plug. The condition of the battery, if of the primary or dry type, may be tested by an amperemeter, or "ammeter", which should read at least six amperes. If it is a wet or storage battery, a voltmeter should be employed, and should show over 3.8 volts. In each case the test should be made quickly. Some voltmeters are so constructed that their indexes come to rest promptly, and they are to be preferred for this reason. Instead of using a voltmeter, one may employ a four-volt test lamp. If this glows, and continues to glow brightly for some five or ten seconds, it may be gathered that the battery contains a sufficient charge, but not otherwise. Use the devices by applying their terminals to those terminals of the battery to which the low-tension wires are connected. If the meter shows nothing at all, reverse the application of its terminals.

If the battery is down, it must either be supplemented by another or recharged, if capable of recharging. Thus, if a two-cell accumulator shows only about three volts (and it should never be allowed to get so low), a single primary battery of about 1.5 volts may be coupled in series with the storage battery and a good current of 4.5 volts obtained. Of course, the right plan is to carry duplicate batteries, so that when one gives out the other may be brought into use. It is just as well to switch over on to the spare battery now and again to make sure that it is in good order, but most of the running should be done on one battery, and then when that is exhausted it can be recharged while the spare is in use. By having a third battery, one can be on charge without depriving the car of its reserve.

Reviving Run-down Batteries.

Although the primary cells are generally reckoned as done for when they have once given out their supply, they can sometimes be temporarily revived to some extent by merely allowing them to stand; and more positively, by making a solution consisting of one part of sulphuric acid and four parts of water, and introducing the same through the venthole of each cell; about a dessertspoonful may be squirted in by means of a small clean oilcan. If the cell will not take the whole charge at once, the operation must be performed in stages. If the venthole is too small, one can make a hole in the marine glue or other material with which the cell is sealed, and introduce the solution through it; the hole being afterwards closed by warming the glue and squeezing it over the hole, or by running in sealing wax. Storage batteries may be temporarily revived by steeping them for several minutes in hot water.

Sometimes it is found that batteries, instead of holding their charges for the proper time, will run down very quickly. This may be due to the primary circuit being left complete accidentally—the driver forgets to switch off after a run. Or it may be due to a short circuit in the wiring; or, again, to some of the paste dropping out of the grids and touching both a positive and a negative plate, thus forming an internal short circuit. Or it may be caused by a leak past the partition between the two cells. If the battery has a transparent celluloid case one can see whether any loose paste is causing a short circuit. To test for a leak past the partition, some of the acid should be poured out of one cell; then, if there is a leak, the acid in the other cell will pass through, and the levels of acid in the two cells will be restored. A leaking partition should receive immediate attention.

Detecting Short Circuits.

Where a short circuit is suspected, it may often be discovered by testing the ignition in the dark, as a spark will be noticed as passing from the defective point. The "short" is most liable to occur in the high-tension circuit, that is, in connection with the wire leading from the coil to the sparking plug; and the short should be looked for while the wire is in the position it generally occupies on the car, as the mere act of moving it in order to make the test above described may prevent the occurrence of the short circuit from which it suffers. It is a great mistake to purchase cheap insulating wire, as a few dischargings of the battery will more than make up the difference between the costs of the cheap and best quality wire. If, on examining the wire, one finds parts that are chafed, they should be carefully bound with insulating tape, and steps should be taken to secure the wire so that further rubbing will be prevented. A better plan is to slip a length of rubber tubing over the wire, or to replace the wire with a new length.

The wires should be kept as free from oil as possible, as oil rots the insulation, and thus invites short circuiting. If the insulation appears to be quite sound, the trouble may arise from breakage of the wire itself. If the wire be passed through the fingers with a bending movement, the break will probably be easily felt; but if not, it may be detected in the case of the primary wire by the voltmeter. The battery, suspected wire, and voltmeter, should be formed into a circuit for the purpose; some tension and twisting movement should be put on the wire during the test. If there is current in the battery, but none can be detected through the wire by the voltmeter, there is evidently a break. The wire should be replaced by another if possible, but if no spare wire is available, the defective one should be cut through at the fault, the insulation slit lengthwise and peeled back for about one inch on each part, and the ends thus bared should be twisted together. The insulation may then be turned back over the joint and the whole bound with insulating tape.

Terminals and Connections.

Though the electricity is willing to adopt all sorts of channels in order to shirk its work, all contacts through which it is intended to pass should be thoroughly clean, and should be scraped with an old knife for this purpose. Avoid using a knife on which you set any value for scraping the terminals of the battery, as you will be very likely to make contact accidentally with both terminals at once, to the great detriment of the blade, not to mention the battery. In order to avoid corrosion, the battery terminals may be anointed with a mixture of vaseline and ammonia.

There are many different devices (also going by the name of terminals) for connecting the wires to the different screws, etc. These are generally more satisfactory than making loops on the ends of the wires themselves, though one has to take care that the attached terminals do not project and touch each other or other metal parts, and so cause short circuits. It is perhaps easier to tell what to avoid than what to do in making terminals out of the ends of the wires themselves. Thus the wire should not be twisted up into an eye of which one part is thicker than another; nor should the eye, when made, be soldered with acid flux, as this brings about corrosion and fracture. If the eye is soldered at all, resin should be used, but the sudden stiffening of the wire by any soldering is also liable to cause breakage.

Probably the simplest way to make an eye is to untwist the wire at a short distance from the end, and then to separate the straightened strands equally by pushing a sharp instrument in between, forming a hole sufficiently large to receive the screw terminal. A stronger eye may be made by baring a good inch of the wire and bending it into a simple loop, and then binding together with fine wire the two parts lying in parallel contact, leaving an eye of suitable size, as before. In securing the one terminal to the other, be careful that no part of the insulation is pinched, as this would tend to prevent perfect contact between the metallic surfaces; at the same time, the insulation should be continued as nearly up to the connection as possible; and for further security, the whole connection may be wrapped with insulating tape. If a detachable plug form part of the primary circuit, and be lost, the two lengths of wire should be coupled together, the switch being relied on for breaking the circuit when required. Or a screw or nail, or a piece of wire doubled up into the form of a rod, will serve as a substitute.

Care of Trembler Points.

Another cause of intermittent firing is looseness of the platinum point on the trembler blade of the contact breaker. The presence of dirty oil on the back of the blade round the platinum is ground for suspecting that the point is loose. Under these circumstances the blade should be detached and laid face downward on a hard surface while the back of the point is riveted over with a light hammer. The faces of the platinum points should make contact squarely with each other; but the passage of the current and the tapping of the one point on the other spoil the surfaces in course of time, and the usual remedy is to file them flat with a thin, watch-maker's file. As platinum, however, is somewhat more expensive than gold, it seems a pity to waste it by filing, and the better plan is to hammer it smooth with a few light and carefully-applied blows. In some cases, too, the distortion of the surfaces can be corrected from time to time by changing over the wires on the battery terminals so as to send the current the reverse way through the points. But if the reversal of the wires is accompanied by the failure of the ignition, or excessive sparking at the contact breaker, they must, of course, be replaced. In any case, no dirt should be allowed to remain between the platinum points, though a drop of oil there is sometimes found to be an advantage rather than otherwise. The points may be cleaned by inserting a thin card or a slip of strong paper between them, and then withdrawing the card while the points are pressed together. Be careful that no particles of paper are left behind, as they will be as bad as, or worse than, the dirt.

Adjusting Contact Breakers.

In adjusting a make-and-break contact breaker one has to see that the cam projection lifts the blade into contact with the screw, and that when the projection has passed, the points are out of contact. Provided the points make a good firm contact, nothing is gained by the excessive bending of the blade, but rather the reverse, as current is wasted by the prolonged contact.

Unscrew the sparking plug and lay it on part of the metal work so that one can see the spark, and so that the terminal end of the plug lies clear of the metal work. Then fix the contact screw at that position which corresponds with the best spark at the plug. Notwithstanding the action of the condenser, a small spark will be noticed as the points at the contact breaker separate. In fact, if no spark shows here it is a pretty sure sign that either the battery is run down or there is a fault in the primary circuit.

Wipe contact breakers are generally self-adjusting by means of a spring. They should, of course, be kept clean, but they should be freely oiled; the reason for this being that if they are run dry the wipe tends to scrape particles off the metallic segment and embed them in the fiber cam, thus constructing a path through which the current will continue to pass after it should be broken, and disturbing the timing of the sparking and wasting the current. Any such particles should be removed; and the metal and fiber surfaces should be kept even with one another, as inequalities frequently cause the wiper to jump, with irregular firing as a result.

Coil Troubles.

When every other part of the ignition system has been proved to be in order, one can only conclude that the trouble is in the coil. This may be due to failure of the insulation. If, on the system being connected up and the contact breaker being worked, a ticking noise be heard in the coil, this is a pretty sure sign of defective insulation. The only remedy is to get the coil repaired by an electrician, preferably the coil-maker himself. The trouble, however, may arise from loose connections at the coil, or from loose strands of wire causing a "short" from one coil terminal to another. These troubles can, of course, be easily remedied if they occur at the exposed ends of the terminals; but if the shorting is between the inside connections, the cover must be carefully removed so as not to break the wires, and as carefully replaced in its proper position after correcting the fault.

If the coil trembler suddenly stops work, it is probably because it has stuck. Should this happen, the trembler may be set in motion again temporarily by unsticking it, but the platinum-pointed screw should be readjusted as soon as possible. The platinum points should be inspected, and, if necessary, cleaned and reshaped; they should stand normally about half a millimeter apart, but it is best to effect the adjustment with the sparking plug where the points can be seen, so that the platinum-pointed screw can be locked at the position which shows the best spark. The tightening of the lock-nut on the screw will generally upset the adjustment somewhat, and this must be allowed for by setting the points a little too close together before finally tightening up. If this adjustment will not cure the trouble, the defect may lie in the loss of elasticity in the spring blades; if so, they must be replaced by new ones.

PART VII.

LOSS OF POWER.

Loss of Power—In ordinary practice the loss of power in a gasolene motor develops rapidly; that is, within a few hours or at most a few days. It would require several years for a motor of modern design and manufacture to wear sufficiently to cause any appreciable falling off in effective work. It must be reasoned, then, that something has gone wrong, more or less suddenly, something that can ordinarily be detected by careful and patient search. This may take several hours, or even a day or two, and can be accomplished only by beginning at the most likely and most frequent cause and going all down the line—by the process of elimination, as in most cases of apparently serious difficulties with the gasolene motor.

Weak batteries, loss of compression and poor carbureter adjustment may be put down as the prime causes of loss of power. It is not difficult to determine the exact state of the ignition system; it is not difficult to adjust a carbureter; and it is not difficult to learn that the motor's compression has fallen off. It is, sometimes, difficult to ascertain the cause of the loss of compression.

It must be remembered, however, that the condition of one of these prime elements bears important relation to the other. For instance, a carbureter cannot be correctly adjusted unless the ignition system is right and the compression is somewhere near normal. Because of this it is essential that the ignition system be given attention first, followed by ascertaining that the compression is good and equal in all the cylinders.

Ignition.

(a) Weak Batteries—Test dry cells to show from 15 to 17 ampères on an ammeter, disregarding voltage. If the batteries show under 5 to 7 ampères, replace with new ones. Possibly only one cell will show depletion, in which case one new cell may effect a remedy, for a time at least. If there are two sets of batteries in the car they can be connected together in series —that is, all the cells connected as if there was but one set— and this will carry the car to a point where new batteries can be secured.

If a storage cell is used, test by connecting one end of a wire to one of the binding posts and snapping the other end across the other binding post. A large, snappy spark will indicate sufficient current; if it is an apparent weak spark, which can easily be determined, the battery needs recharging.

It is well to know that dry cells can be obtained at almost any telephone office in the country, so that under ordinary circumstances the motorist can run his car to one of these stations.

(b) Timer Slipped—This retards the ignition and usually causes overheating of the motor. The location of the timer in relation to the shaft to which it is attached should be marked, so as to be replaced easily. Also, the owner should know just where the spark lever should be on the quadrant when the piston is at the top of the compression stroke, and when contact on the timer is made. Sometimes the slipping may be found to have occurred at the connections between the hand lever and the timer. Look these over and if possible take up all slack, so as to make the movement of the timer through the spark lever positive.

(c) Plugs, Fouled or Short Circuited—Clean the plugs by immersing in gasolene and cutting the carbon deposits off with a knife. At the same time see that the points are 1/32-inch apart—no more, no less. Accumulated oil will cause a short circuit, as will carbon deposits or a cracked or chipped porcelain.

(d) Timer Gummed—Unless a timer is cleaned occasionally the old grease or oil will become gummed and saturated with metal filings caused by wear. This will cause a loss of some of the current and result in lag in the ignition; consequently a feeble impulse in one or more cylinders. Likewise a magneto must be kept clean in order to transmit current. A timer should be cleaned with gasolene and after dried of all the gasolene should be packed in hard grease, which not only remains as a lubricant but will tend to prevent dust from reaching the contact points.

(e) Poor Contact on Timer or Magneto—Where a timer is used, not infrequently the primary wire is not fitted with terminals to attach to the binding posts on the timer and the coil, the wires of several strands being attached direct. The movement of the timer in retarding and advancing the spark gradually breaks these little strands, until perhaps, only one or two remain—and one or two are not sufficient to carry current. In other cases the primary wires at the timer become oil-soaked and much current is lost. Poor contact at the timer, magneto, coil, battery, switch or plug will prevent a full flow of current and interrupt proper ignition of the gases in the cylinders.

(f) Oil-soaked Secondary Wires—Keep the wires leading to the plugs, in particular, and in fact any wires, free from oil and dirt, otherwise more or less of the circuit will be lost.

Loss of Compression.

(a) Valves Fouled; Not Seating—If the motor shows loss of compression, look first to the condition of the valves; probably they do not seat properly and closely and must be ground. This should be done promptly. Too much lubrication—possibly in combination with a poor mixture—causes this state of affairs. In cities, where speed is restricted and where the motorist is tempted to jog along with a low charge of gas and a high spark, the heat from the explosion is not sufficient to burn the excess of oil and the valves soon become coated, preventing them from seating and permitting the loss of compression.

(b) Nuts for Valve Cages not Tight—In valve-in-the-head motors, where cages are employed to form the valve seat and carry the valve and stem, the ring nut used to hold the cage down on its seat may not be set down tight, thus permitting compression to become weak. When the motor is hot, after two or three hours' use, set the nuts down. Treat valve nuts in T-head motors the same way. Where the threads have spread or become worn through constant removal, make a thin paste of litharge and glycerin and rub on the threads. Set the ring or nut down tight and let stand over night for the litharge to harden. It might be stated here that cracks, small holes, etc., may be thoroughly closed by the use of litharge in this form.

(c) Valve Spring Weak—Where a valve spring has become weakened, a temporary repair may be made by building up with iron washers that will fit over the valve stem and cover the spring, care being taken that the washers do not bind the valve stem or prevent its free working.

(d) Valve Spring Broken—If a valve spring breaks, place an iron washer between the pieces of spring—over the valve stem, of course—and a splendid emergency job will have been accomplished, one that will last indefinitely.

(e) Air Leak at Plug—This can be detected, usually, by placing the hand near the plug, when escaping air or gas can be felt. Or, pour a little oil around the plug while the motor is running and the leak will be immediately noticed by the oil bubbling. A leaky valve may be detected in the same manner. If the plug has a shoulder, a copper gasket can be inserted between the shoulder and the cylinder. If there is no shoulder, litharge and glycerine in a paste can be used on the threads to stop the leak.

(f) Rings Stuck—Over-lubrication will cause the oil to settle under the rings on the piston and eventually stick them to the piston, permitting the gas to escape past the rings. Inject a couple of teaspoonfuls of kerosene in each cylinder and permit it to stand over night. This will loosen the rings effectually. Better still, do not over-lubricate and the rings will not stick; too much lubrication will cause as much trouble—but not as much damage—as an insufficient supply.

(g) Broken Ring—If a ring breaks, its springiness is gone and the gases will escape past. The only remedy is a new ring A metallic knock sometimes will denote a broken ring.

(h) Ring Slots in Line—Where rings are not pinned in place, it is possible for the slots at the ends to "get in line," and under such circumstances gases will escape. If the rings are free they will right themselves. This is an unlikely trouble, however.

(i) Lack of Pushrod Clearance—Be sure there is clearance between the pushrods and valve stems, otherwise the valves will be held open slightly but sufficiently to cause loss of compression. This is apt to occur after valve grinding and the valve has been lowered a trifle through grinding. Give some clearance, as a temporary relief, but ascertain from the maker of the car the right amount to give proper valve lift.

(j) Lack of Lubrication—Oil fills the space between the cylinder walls and rings and piston. Lack of oil will permit some gas to escape.

(k) Leak at Gasket—Where cylinder heads are detachable, and where gaskets are used, a leak is very possible. A new gasket should be put in, using shellac on either side to cement it to the iron.

(l) Rocker Shaft Worn or Loose—In motors fitted with make-and-break ignition the rocker shaft may have become worn, or the rocker shaft barrel loosened, permitting loss of compression. Usually the remedy for the first named is either a new shaft or new mica insulation, while a copper gasket can be used over the barrel.

(m) Valve Stem Bent—A bent valve stem will prevent the valves from properly opening and closing by sticking and thus cause loss of compression. It can be heated and straightened for a temporary repair, but a new one is the surest remedy. If bent only slightly a little filing and finishing with fine emery cloth will prove effective for a temporary job. Where a valve stem has been straightened it is best to put it in a lathe to be trued up and then ground to fit the valve seat.

(n) Cylinders or Rings Out of True—In horizontal motors in particular, where one side of the piston rests on one side of the cylinder, these parts are liable to "wear oval." This is not apt to occur in a vertical motor. To effectually remedy this the cylinders must be reground and new pistons and rings fitted.

Mixture.

(a) Lack of Gasolene—Insufficient supply of gasolene at the spray nozzle—through clogging by sediment or dirt, or lack of pressure in pressure-feed systems—will cause a loss of power, particularly in hill-climbing or through heavy roads. Water in the gasolene will sometimes slightly restrict the flow, which should at all times be free. The remedy is a thorough cleaning of the fuel line.

(b) Surplus of Gasolene—Too much gasolene, through too great an opening of the needle valve of the carbureter will tend to choke the motor, particularly upon opening the throttle suddenly, and cause a sluggish-running motor. It will also heat the motor. If it is a case of too little or too much gasolene, readjust the carbureter, as per direction elsewhere.

(c) Float Level Too High—If the level of the gasolene in the carbureter is such as to be more than just below the top of the spray nozzle—about 1/32 to 1/16-inch in most carbureters—the mixture will be too heavy and cause sluggish running of the motor—if too low, the feed will be insufficient and will cause a loss of power at normal speeds and missing at high motor speeds. Where the float level is too low the valve shuts off too soon. With the gasolene level wrong it is impossible to properly adjust the carbureter, inasmuch as the tendency is to increase the fuel supply through opening the needle valve, which, while it may result in a correct mixture at some particular motor speed may be too rich at another. To correctly adjust a carbureter it is necessary to have the gasolene level right and to also have the ignition in good working order.

(d) Auxiliary Air Valve Spring Broken—Should the air valve spring in the carbureter be broken—which is not likely, however—the motor will be permitted to take in a surplus of air. This will in all probability be known by the motor missing if it keeps on running, which is doubtful. A case was known, however, where the air valve spring was entirely gone and still the motor would run, although it was hard to start and did not develop power. Should the air valve slip out of place or be broken the effect on the motor would be similar to that in the case of a broken spring.

Other Causes.

(a) Lack of Water Circulation—Insufficient supply of water in the cooling system, or poor water circulation, causing overheating or a tendency to overheat, will permit the cylinders and pistons to expand and to bind sufficiently to precipitate a loss of power. This will in all likelihood be preceded by a decided knocking, especially if the lubrication is not excessive.

(b) Intake Restricted—Where a car has been driven through dusty or muddy roads, the gradual accumulation of dirt in the intake pipe because of the absence of a pan under the motor, for instance, will settle in the pipe and cause a restriction that will act as a throttle. This can be remedied only by removing the pipe and cleaning by running a gasolene-soaked cloth through it.

(c) Throttle Connections Slipped—See that the connections between the throttle lever and the valve in the carbureter have not slipped and permitted the throttle to become partially closed. This is a not infrequent cause of the apparent lack of power.

(d) Muffler or Exhaust Pipe Clogged—A restricted muffler or exhaust pipe will pull down the power to a remarkable degree. If a cut-out is fitted to the exhaust system it will be easy to discover, with this open, if the motor seems to develop its full power. If it shows a falling off of power when closed the exhaust pipe and muffler should be cleaned. They should be taken down, soaked in kerosene and washed out with gasolene. Be sure, however, to see that the gasolene has been permitted to evaporate before attaching to the car and starting the motor, else a bad explosion may result. They should be permitted to stand all night and in a position so as to drain well.

(e) Too Heavy Load—If the car is loaded beyond its normal capacity it is not unlikely there will be a falling off in apparent power. Load the car to its normal capacity and see if there is any appreciable difference in the work of the motor.

(f) Bind on Running Gear or Transmission—Gummed axle bearings, dry differential or transmission, bent axle or steering knuckles, motor or transmission out of line, brakes binding or partially set, will cause loss of power. In searching for the cause it will be well to push the car along the floor to see if it runs freely, and that there is nothing materially wrong with the running gear. If it pushes hard it will be necessary to trace the trouble and remedy it.

(g) Soft Tires—Soft tires will make a car push extremely hard, either by hand or by motor power. Before trying the car to see how the running gear works, be sure the tires are pumped hard.

(h) Stiff Valve Springs—Where suction valves are used and a change in the springs has been made, possibly one that is too strong has been used. This will prevent a full charge of gas from entering the cylinders and thus the force of the explosion will be materially weakened. This cannot occur, however, unless some change has been made in the springs.

(i) Quality of Fuel—Fuel has much to do with the power that can be obtained from a gasolene motor, but if a carbureter is adjusted for certain grades the difference will hardly be perceptible. It is a mistake to suppose that a grade of gasolene of high test will give more power; as a matter of fact there are more heat units in a given quantity, in bulk, of the lower grades, but unless the carbureter is properly adjusted these heat units in the lower grades cannot be turned into working agents as readily as can those in the higher grades. With the lower grades of gasolene more heat is required to volatilize the gasolene than with the higher grades.

(j) Cold Motor—When a motor is extremely cold, particularly if the gasolene supply at the needle valve is cut down to a pretty fine point, the gasolene cannot be volatilized or made into gas and the actual result is a very light charge. In this case it is well, when the motor shows loss of power and misses, to run the motor with a later spark and a larger charge of gas until the motor has had an opportunity to become warm and to help volatilize the gasolene.

PART VIII.

CARE AND MAINTENANCE.

Care and Maintenance—Private Housing—The private car house or garage should, if possible, be constructed of brick, stone or cement, though where cost is a prime consideration, very serviceable wooden and corrugated iron houses can be built. The house should be large enough to provide a space of at least four feet all round the car.

There should be large doors at each end of the house if space permits, so that the car may be run in one way and out the other. This will save a lot of time and trouble in reversing.

The floor should be of concrete, and care should be taken to avoid nooks and crannies, into which small parts can run and hide, if accidentally dropped. In the middle of the floor a pit should be dug. This should measure about 3 ft. 6 in. wide, 4 ft. deep, and 6 ft. or more long, according to the size of the car. Steps should lead down into it at each end, and a strong cover must be provided. The edge of the pit should have a projecting ridge to prevent the wheels of the car being accidentally moved over the pit, and also to prevent other things running into it. The pit, as well as the floor of the house, should be drained.

Light and Warmth.

Light is best admitted through windows in the roof, and these should be made to open and close, or other ample means of ventilation should be provided. If a current of electricity can be laid on to the garage, it will be found a great advantage in several ways. In the first place it affords a very convenient and safe means of lighting at night. Besides handlights that can be carried about, a number of fixed sockets for the electric lamps should be provided on the walls, and also in the pit. The electric current will also be useful in charging the batteries, especially if the car is an electric one.

A good supply of water should be laid on for cleaning purposes, and the soft rainwater falling on the roof should be collected in a covered tank, as soft water should always be used in the radiator. The water should be drawn off as clear as possible, and passed through a fine strainer into the radiator.

The warming of the house requires careful attention. It is not advisable to use a coal fire or oilstove inside the house on account of the flame. A very high temperature is not desirable; provided it is well above freezing, that is enough, though it is always safest to run off the circulating water, in case the heating apparatus break down. So far as the tires are concerned, the atmosphere of the house should be neither too hot nor too dry; nor, for that matter, too light.

A workbench should be erected near one corner of the house, and if it can be supplemented by a small lathe so much the better. If the car is provided with a detachable top for the body, a pulley should be hung from the middle of the roof, so that the top may be manipulated easily, and suspended clear when out of use.

Cleaning.

On returning from a dirty run the mud may be washed off the car by carefully turning the hose on it. The painted work may be afterward dried with a soft clean sponge, and be polished with a leather in the usual way. In using the hose, care should be taken to keep the water and grit out of the bearings and other working parts as much as possible. The tires should be wiped clean and dried. See that they are well inflated, and that no water gets in to rust the rims and rot the canvas. The exterior of the engine, gear, etc., may best be cleaned by a good-sized paint brush dipped in kerosene. If the leathers of the clutch, brakes or pump get too greasy, they may be cleansed by washing with waste gasolene. The clutch leather should not be allowed to get dry; on the contrary, it should be kept moist with special oil, evenly applied, and preferably allowed to soak in over night.

It is worth while giving the chains of chain-driven cars a good deal more attention than they generally receive. They should be taken off occasionally and thoroughly cleansed in a bath of kerosene. Then they should be hung up to drain, and subsequently be dipped in a bath of melted tallow, which may contain a fair proportion of graphite. The tallow should be no hotter than is required to keep it liquid. After the chains have been stirred about in the tallow, so as to work it into the joints, they should be wiped, to remove the surplus grease, and allowed to cool. It is a good plan to keep two sets of chains, so that while one set is in use, plenty of time will be available for treating the other.

The muffler should be cleaned out occasionally to prevent the deposits therein accumulating to such an extent as to choke the passages, and so put back pressure on the motor.

Care of the Hands.

While on the subject of cleaning it may be as well to give here one or two hints as to cleaning the hands. Before starting to do anything to a motor car, it is a good plan to fill the nails and the crevices around the same with soap, and the fingers also may be rubbed over with the same material. This prevents the dirt securing positions from which it is most difficult to dislodge it. A great deal of the dirt that does adhere may be removed by rinsing the hands in kerosene or stale gasolene. To rub the hands in vaseline and put a few drops of ammonia into the hot washing water is a useful plan. Many have also found soft soap, pumicestone soap, and some of the advertised preparations useful for cleaning the hands. Gasolene, even if stale, comes in handy for removing grease spots from the clothes. A piece of flannel should be moistened with the gasolene, and a ring described with it round the spot, to prevent the latter spreading. Then a second application of the liquid should be made, first holding the moistened flannel on the spot for a few moments and then rubbing it vigorously. The odor very quickly passes off.

Lubricating.

All the rotating and rubbing surfaces on the motor require lubrication, except leather brake bands, leather pump tire, and

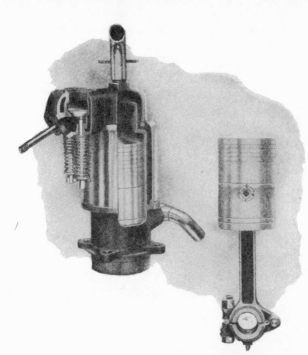

Cadillac "Thirty" Cylinder and Piston.

Cadillac "Thirty" Steering Gear.   Cadillac "Thirty" Transmission.

the stems of the inlet and exhaust valves. Besides the motor itself, the steering sockets, connections, worm and column bearings require attention; also the bearings of the road wheels, the transmission gearing and levers, the balance gear, and the starting apparatus. The pump and radiator fan bearings must not be overlooked. A new car requires more lubricating during the first 200 or 300 miles, while it is settling down, than it does afterwards. If the engine appears sluggish, it is sometimes due to lack of lubrication; a little extra oil will often help in hill-climbing. The dirty oil which accumulates in the crank case should be run off occasionally, and every few hundred miles the oil pipes and bearings should be cleansed out with kerosene, the engine run for half a minute or so in this way, and then the kerosene run off and full doses of proper lubricating oil administered. When using the kerosene, make sure that it runs through. If a pipe gets choked it should be blown clear, or a wire pushed through it.

While it is bad economy to stint the lubricating oil, it is a very common fault to use a great deal too much. This is not only wasteful, but tends to foul the valves, sparking plugs, and platinum contacts. Further, it has a prejudicial effect in creating a cloud of evil blue smoke. The driver should keep a look-out to see that he is not thus polluting the atmosphere and bringing motoring into evil repute. He should also be careful to close his lubricators when stopping, as otherwise the cloud will be apparent when restarting, even though the lubricators may be correctly adjusted for running.

Adjusting.

"Little and often" is an excellent motto in the care of motor cars, the "little" being a consequence of the "often." The great thing is to give the attention regularly. All working parts should be adjusted to move freely but without shake. This insures the highest efficiency and absence of noise. Spring washers are often useful in attaining these results where proper means are not provided for adjustment. All nuts used for positive gripping purposes should be secured by castle locknuts, with split pins passing through a hole in the bolt and through the slots in the nut.

Adjustable Bearings.

As a rule, the owner will do well not to attempt the adjustment of plain and roller bearings. Ball bearings are comparatively easy to adjust, if provision is made for adjustment. At one end will be found a locknut, and on the same screw a cone. When the locknut is released the cone may be screwed along the spindle either into or out of the bearing. It should be screwed in until it will go no further without using force, then it should be unscrewed about half a turn. Now, if the locknut be retightened, it will probably be found that the bearing will work freely and without shake. It is better to have just a perceptible shake than to have a bearing too tight, and the final tightening of the locknut will usually tighten the bearing itself a little, owing to slackness in the screw threads.

A scrunching noise in a bearing should receive immediate attention, the bearing being taken apart in order to discover the cause. It may be found to be due merely to the presence of some grit, though that is bad enough. In this case a thorough cleansing of the bearing and lubrication will cure the trouble. If one of the balls is found to be broken, all the bits must be removed and a new ball inserted. But unless a new one of exactly the right size can be procured, it is best to run the bearing with the ball short for the time being; as, should the new ball be a shade too large, it will also certainly cause trouble. When the bearing is apart the cones and cups should be carefully examined for scores and cracks, as if these are found, the parts affected should be renewed at the earliest opportunity. In some cases, where the damage to the bearing parts is serious, it is best to remove the balls and let the bearing run on the plain surfaces as far as the nearest point available for repairs. If a wheel spindle has been cut into so as to weaken it materially, the load should be lightened as much as possible, or the run discontinued entirely, pending repairs.

A car should not be run with either the wheel bearings or

the steering crossbar joints very slack, as the wheels will wobble under these conditions, and the bearings and tires will get badly worn.

Brake Treatment.

The adjustment of the brakes is even more important than that of the bearings. They require treating according to their individual construction. Two points, however, should be borne in mind: First, that the pedal or hand lever should not be at the limit of its stroke, even when the brake is hard on; and second, that the braking surfaces should not rub anywhere when the brake is off.

Charging Batteries.

As there are now many stations where one can get batteries charged at a small expense, it seems hardly worth while troubling to do one's own charging if this involves putting in a plant for the purpose. But where a suitable source of electricity is available, it is a great thing to be able to keep the voltage well over 4; and where no charging station is at hand, it may be almost necessary to do the work oneself. And here the reader may be reminded that if he finds himself in a strange place where no one undertakes recharging, and where no wet cells are to be bought, dry batteries can often be purchased at the local hardware store; and one or two of these may be coupled in series with the expiring accumulators on the car, or a complete set may be secured to do the work alone. Failing this, you may have the good luck to get recharged from the generating plant of some large private installation.

The current for recharging may be obtained from a suitable dynamo (either directly or through an electric lighting system) or from a primary battery.

Recharging from a Strange Supply.

If the recharging is to be done from a dynamo constructed for the purpose, or from a specially-designed switchboard worked on the local electric lighting system, the job will be simple enough. But if you want to charge up from a strange supply, the first thing to do is to inquire whether it is a continuous or an alternating current, and what is the voltage. We will suppose the current to be continuous, and of 110 volts.

The charging rate should be marked on the battery case. Usually it will not be over two ampères, but this may generally be exceeded by fifty per cent. if time is short. A safe charging rate may generally be found by dividing the ampère hourage of the battery by 10. A 16 c. p. (candle power) lamp will pass about half an ampère, and a 32 c. p. lamp will pass about one ampère, so a switch controlling four of the former or two of the latter lamps should be found. Two of the former or one of the latter will be better if the time can be af-

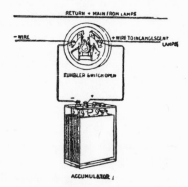

Fig. 1.—Charging from Ordinary Switch, Open.

forded, as slow charging at a low ampèrage is best for the battery, and conduces to long running. A six 16 c. p. or three 32 c. p. lamp switch may be used if one is in a hurry. The lamps are generally marked with their candle-power and can be disconnected from their sockets by simple twisting and withdrawing action.

The switch must be put into the off position (which will put the lamps out, so have another light handy), and must be kept in this position during the whole process. See Fig. 1. If the switch were closed it would short circuit the battery; and, besides wasting a lot of current, would damage the plates.

Pole Finding.

As charging is opposite to working, the positive pole of the charging apparatus must be coupled up to the positive pole of the accumulator, during charging. To find which pole is which in the switch, unscrew the cover, and connect separate wires to the terminals. Now take a slip of pole-finding paper, wet it thoroughly, and lay the free ends of the two wires on it, about half an inch apart. The paper will usually turn red around the end of the negative wire, but read the directions on the packet of papers as they do not all work alike.

If you have no pole-finding paper, drop a little vinegar into a glass of water, and hold the ends of the wires about ¼ in.

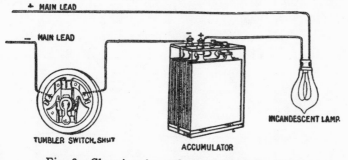

Fig. 2.—Charging from Ordinary Switch, Shut.

apart in the water thus acidulated. Bubbles will be seen rising from the end of the negative wire. Bubbles may come from both wires, but if so, they will come faster from one (the negative) than from the other.

The two wires can now be coupled up to the terminals of similar polarity respectively on the battery; and as soon as the circuit is completed by so doing, the lamps will light up again.

Or one of the wires leading to the switch may be severed, and the ends thus made be connected to the terminals, positive to positive and negative to negative, as before. (Fig. 2.) This allows the switch to be used in the ordinary way; but, of course, the battery will not be charging when the switch is "off."

Instead of coupling up to a switch, one may employ an adapter. This is a fitting for attaching to a lamp socket in place of the lamp. The displaced lamp should be fitted into a socket comprised in the adapter, and the polarity of the wires having been ascertained, the positive wire is coupled to the positive terminal of the accumulator, and the negative to the negative, as before.

With a current of more than 110 volts, the number of 16 c. p. lamps should be increased, about in the proportion of one lamp to thirty volts. If the lighting system is worked on an alternating current, it will be necessary to employ a rectifier to transform the current into a continuous one. Some of the charging dynamos are made to be driven by water pressure from the house supply.

Charging from a Primary Battery.

But where neither electric lighting nor water is laid on to

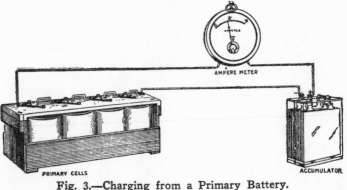

PRIMARY CELLS   ACCUMULATOR

Fig. 3.—Charging from a Primary Battery.

the house, one can use a large primary battery. When employing this system an ammeter should be introduced into the circuit; and the zincs should be let down into the liquid just so far that the required number of ampères is shown on the meter. The zincs should be lowered from time to time to keep up the number of ampères. Instead of moving the zincs, a small resistance may be introduced into the circuit and adjusted as required. Some of these primary batteries should be very carefully handled, as the liquids employed therein are highly corrosive. They require replenishing from time to time, and the zincs should be entirely withdrawn while the battery is not in use.

Whatever system of charging is adopted, the vent plugs should be removed from the accumulators, to allow free escape of the generated gases, during the process. The time occupied in charging naturally varies, but six hours to eight hours may be taken as an average. The battery should be disconnected soon after the electrolyte begins to bubble, and the voltmeter should then show a reading of at least 4.4. Sometimes it may show as much as 5.0, but the pressure will soon drop to an orthodox level when the accumulator is put to work. Wipe the case quite dry, vaseline the terminals, and replace the vent plugs before returning the battery to its position in the car.

Water Circulation.

A few hints may be given here on the subject of circulation. If the pump is driven by frictional contact with the flywheel, the spring should be adjusted so that it will just prevent slipping in the drive; greater tension will only have the effect of wearing out the bearings without any improved result. If it is suspected that the water is not circulating properly, one of the upper connections may be opened, when, if the water spurts out, it may be concluded that the circulation is in action. Some cars are now fitted with a manometer, which indicates the circulation of the water visibly. When one has become accustomed to a particular car, the condition of the circulation can be inferred from the temperatures of the inlet and outlet water pipes, as tested by the hand. If the water is not circulating satisfactorily the trouble will almost certainly arise from the pump. This should be taken to pieces and thoroughly cleaned, and any defect that may be found should be remedied as far as possible.

If the water is boiling, and one wishes to replace it with cold, the operation should be performed gradually. Do not simply run off the boiling water and then fill up with cold, but make the change in easy stages. The advice given elsewhere to empty the circulating tank after each run in cold weather will bear repeating, but the risk of freezing may be reduced by mixing glycerine with the water in the proportion of one of the former to two or three of the latter (or some other anti-freezing mixture). Sometimes the pipes will become furred, and the cooling effect of the water thereby reduced, by reason both of the diminished capacity for water and the increased thickness of the containing walls. The fur may be dissolved by introducing a quantity of some strong alkali, such as caustic soda, into the cooling water. Two or three applications may be made until the water comes away practically clean.

If one of the pipes break, a temporary repair may be effected by slipping a length of rubber tubing over the broken ends, and binding tightly with wire. If the pipe has broken off close to one end, a reunion can sometimes be effected by tapering down the end of the pipe and somewhat enlarging the hole it ought to communicate with. The end of the pipe is then forced into the hole and tied in position, and the joint completed with red lead and insulating tape. This is a rather difficult repair, and should be superseded by a workshop job as soon as possible.

The Care of Tires.

One of the great advantages of pneumatic tires is that their strength of spring can be adjusted to the work they have to do, and they should be inflated to such a pressure that they will give only slightly when they rest under the weight of the car and passengers. So long as these conditions continue all is well. Occasional reinflation may be necessary. A speedy deflation demands instant attention. Pneumatic tires cost quite enough while doing their work, but to drive a car with a deflated tire is ruinous.

Directly a tire goes down the car should be stopped, and the cause ascertained. In case of doubt, the first thing to do **is to reinflate, and then ascertain if the valve is leaking, by** placing a film of moisture over the orifice at the exposed end. If this is found to be the seat of the trouble, the valve should be tightened up or repaired, as the case may require. But unless the valve can be dealt with from the outside, the next step is to jack up the wheel and clean the outside of the tire cover. Then the tire must be completely deflated, when it may be opened.

Removing the Cover.

The nuts holding down the valve, and the security bolts, must be screwed nearly off, and the valve and bolts pushed well back into the tire. The side of the cover nearer to you should then be pressed away from you all round the wheel, so as to unstick the edge, bead, or rib of the cover from the edge of the rim. Now take two tire levers and thrust them down between the edges of the cover and rim, about nine inches apart. Do not push the levers too far in or they may damage the air tube. Press down the outer ends of the levers, so as to raise the edge of the cover above the edge of the rim. If you have a helper, let him insert a third lever, about nine inches beyond the second, and pull it down like the others. But if you are alone on the job, pull the first lever down to the vertical and secure it by a loop to one of the spokes. The loop should be put around the spoke before pulling the lever down. Having secured the first lever, move the second further along and pull it down again. Quite a number of special tire levers have been introduced, some of which are much easier to manipulate than the ordinary bar levers. Repeat the levering until a good portion of the cover has been pried over the edge of the rim; the rest can be worked out by hand. The valve may now be completely removed from the rim, and the air tube withdrawn from the cover.

It may be that there is a leak between the head of the valve and the air tube, and this may generally be cured by tightening the nut which secures the valve to the tube.

In cleaning the cover, however, one may have come across a cut, or the head of a nail, or other interesting object, indicating a puncture, and the interior of the cover should be carefully examined to see if any nails or the like are projecting through the inner surface, and also to see whether any parts of the lining are discolored by the penetration of wet through cuts in the rubber. Wet rots the canvas very quickly, and such spots should be treated both from without and from within.

Advantage of Spare Tubes.

Repairing a puncture in a motor car tire is a much more serious affair than dealing with a similar trouble in a bicycle tire; and, even with light car tires, unless the patching process is very carefully and patiently carried out, the result will not be satisfactory. Hence it is much better to carry one or two spare tubes, and insert one of these, than to attempt to execute a repair by the roadside.

Vulcanized Tire Repairs.

The unsatisfactory results too frequently attaching to attempts to repair motor car tires by the ordinary patching system have led to the introduction of small vulcanizing plants, some of which are portable enough to be carried on a car, and indeed are specially constructed with a view to this. The system differs essentially from patching, in that the damaged part is remade instead of merely repaired. In the case of a punctured air tube, the rubber round the hole is cut away so as to form a beveled or concave seating extending right through the wall of the tube. This gives a fresh surface of large area. The cutting may be effected by gouging, or by folding the tube so as to bring the puncture to a corner, and then snipping off the corner with a pair of sharp scissors. The tool should be wetted, as rubber cuts much more easily when wet than when dry. The fresh surface is then roughened by rubbing with sandpaper or a small rasp to facilitate penetration by the flux, which is next applied thereto. This flux is a solution of raw rubber mixed with sulphur and other ingredients. When the first coat of flux becomes sticky, a second may be applied, and this should also be allowed to reach the "tacky" stage before the next operation is proceeded with.

It is convenient while doing this part of the work to tie the air tube down flat, as, for example, across the top of a wheel with a sound tire.

The next thing to do is to fill up the enlarged hole with rubber compound, which is a similar material to the flux, but in a plastic or putty-like state. It is well to warm the compound, as by dabbing it on the vulcanizer, before kneading it into place. The compound should be pressed well in, and rather more than enough applied. The surplus should be trimmed off with a wet, sharp knife, great care being taken not to cut the tube in so doing.

A typical apparatus consists of a small brass boiler with vertical fire tubes. One side of the boiler is made flat to adapt it to the vulcanizing of air tubes; the opposite side is concaved to suit the contour of the outer surface of the purchaser's tire covers. The water is filled into the boiler through an orifice at the top until it runs out at the blow-off cock, which also forms part of the steam pressure gauge on the boiler. The furnace consists of a cylindrical alcohol lamp. The spirit is soaked up by cotton-wool located in the cylinder under a wire gauze burning surface. The lamp telescopes into the lower part of the boiler, and the heat can be regulated by pushing in and drawing out a sliding sleeve or extinguisher to a greater or less extent. A detachable metal arm is secured to the upper part of the boiler, and forms a handle by which the vulcanizer can be moved about. The bent outer end of the arm forms a bracket, and carries a screw between the end of which and the flat surface of the boiler the air tube is gripped during the vulcanizing process. A metal plate and a block of wood or vulcanized fiber are introduced between the point of the screw and the air tube. The vulcanizer is fitted with a socket whereby it can be mounted on the rear light lamp-bracket when repairing air tubes, and with a detachable chain device whereby it may be secured directly to the wheel in the case of repairing a cut cover.

It should be clearly understood that the boiler is employed simply because it provides the most convenient method for securing the necessary heat. There is no magic in the heat being produced by steam. Further, the steam pressure has nothing to do with the pressure exerted on the tube or cover under repair. The pressure of the steam is merely useful as indicating in a convenient manner certain temperatures corresponding thereto. As it takes some ten or fifteen minutes to raise cold water to the necessary steam pressure of 50 lbs. to the square inch (corresponding to a good vulcanizing temperature of about 281° F.), it is advisable to start the boiler before preparing the punctured part of the air tube, and also to use warm water (as from the radiator) instead of cold.

The injured tube having been treated as above described, and the indicator on the boiler showing 50 lbs. pressure, a piece of tissue paper or linen, rather larger than the flat surface of the boiler, is laid on the part of the tube, which is them pressed flat against the boiler by means of the screw and plates. The screw should be turned by the fingers only; this will give sufficient pressure. The paper or linen prevents the rubber compound sticking to the surface of the boiler. The wood or fiber plate should not be so large as to reach and pinch the edges of the air tube. If the wound is a large one, instead of a mere puncture, it should be treated in a similar way; but it is then as well to insert a piece of tissue paper in the air tube, so that the repaired part shall not stick to the opposite wall when vulcanized. After about a quarter of an hour the sulphur will be thoroughly melted, and the raw rubber compound thereby vulcanized.

The tube may now be removed from the vulcanizer, and if the thumb-nail be dug into the repaired part, the impression should quickly disappear when the nail is removed, otherwise the vulcanizing should be carried on for a few minutes longer. The time varies with the thickness of the article being treated, not with the size of the surface. A gash will take no longer to vulcanize than a puncture, but a thick tube should be given about twenty minutes instead of fifteen.

Cuts in the cover are treated substantially in the same way. The rubber should be cut away around the injury right down to the first canvas, and at such an angle as to expose a large surface of fresh rubber around it. It is then rasped and treated with one or two coats of flux, and after the last of these has become tacky, the hole is filled up with compound, well pressed in with a roller tool provided for the purpose, and pared off flush with the surface of the cover. Meanwhile the vulcanizer has been getting up steam on the bracket. The damaged portion of the cover is brought to the back or front of the wheel. The injury is covered with paper or linen, and the vulcanizer is secured to the wheel, with the concave side to the injury, by means of a chain which should be screwed up fairly tight, but not so as to indent the cover materially. Owing to the greater thickness of the material, the heat will have some difficulty in penetrating it. A pressure of 60 lbs. may be used for about fifteen minutes, twenty minutes being necessary for 50 lbs. The cover should be perfectly dry, and the dryness may generally be obtained by putting the vulcanizer in position before the required pressure has been obtained, so that the moisture may be evaporated before the 50 lbs. or 60 lbs. has been reached, and before the vulcanizing has commenced. A pad of cloth should be placed temporarily between the cover and vulcanizer to let the damp vapor escape. Special adapters can be obtained for covers of special formation.

The above described vulcanizer weighs about 10 lbs. More elaborate ones are made for garage use, and are provided with means for repairing burst covers. In the case of an ordinary burst, the cover should be turned inside out, and a large piece of the lining should be cut away right across the inside of the cover. Then the material should be cut away in layers extending to the depth of one canvas each. The portions of canvas cut away should be of rectangular form with rounded corners, and each layer should measure about one and a half to two inches less in length and breadth than the one previously removed. The last layer of canvas should not be cut out, but should be left bare to the extent of about one inch all round the burst. During this operation the portions of fresh canvas should be cut to the shapes of those detached, and saturated with the flux, successive coats being applied and allowed to get "tacky" until a substantial film of rubber is left on both the surfaces. The steps cut in the cover should be coated with flux in the same way. The cover is now turned back again outside out. The wound in the tread is treated as before described, and the patches of canvas are laid in position, and pressed down with the roller. The last piece should be considerably larger than the others, and as it is to replace the damaged portion of the lining, it should be solutioned on the back only. When this is in place, the cover is put in the vulcanizer between two properly shaped steam containers, one inside and the other out, and it is bound down tightly to the inner container by a strip of webbing wound on spirally. The parts are gripped thus, and a pressure of 60 lbs. is kept up for about twenty-five minutes, or longer if necessary.

Air tubes may be joined, and other jobs done in a substantially similar manner.

Repairs by Patching.

In the absence of a sound spare tube and of a vulcanizer, the patching process will have to be resorted to. The air tube should be examined for one or more punctures. If the trouble cannot be ascertained by mere inspection, the tube should be reinflated lightly, and immersed and stretched, bit by bit, in a large bowl of water, when the seat of the injury will be discovered by a stream of bubbles issuing from the puncture.

Draw a ring on the tube, concentrically with the puncture, with an indelible ink pencil. As this is to serve as a guide to the position of the hole during the subsequent operations, it should be rather larger than the patch to be applied. The surface around the puncture and within the ring must be thoroughly cleaned. Gasolene is very useful for cleaning off the sulphur and preparing the rubber for the solution. A block of sulphur is also handy; but the usual process is to wrap a piece of glass paper round something hard, such as the chalk case, and rub the tube clean around the seat of the injury. When all the sulphur has been removed, a thin film of indiarubber solution should be spread on the prepared surface. The area of the film should be sufficient to extend well beyond the edges of the patch to be applied. This film should be allowed five or ten minutes to dry, and another spread over it, and subsequently a third. If the films of solution are exposed to the direct rays of the sun they will dry quickly.

One of the rubber patches in the repair outfit should be chosen according to its size, and this also should be cleaned and given three coats of solution, each being thoroughly dry before the next is applied. If the patch shows an irresistible desire to curl up, encourage it to embrace a fixed rod of suitable diameter, so that it shall not roll about and get covered with dust, etc. The patch should then be carefully laid on the solutioned part of the tube, which should be quite empty of air at the time. The patch should be firmly pressed down on the tube, the pressure being applied from the center outward, so as to drive out any bubbles of air that may have been caught between the patch and the tube. The patched portion of the tube may be laid between two flat plates and moderate pressure applied, as by a vise or a weight. When the patch is well set, it should be further secured by a much larger canvas-backed patch solutioned on in a similar way, the canvas being outward.

If the puncturing object has penetrated right through the tube, of course both holes will require mending; and a second hole should always be carefully looked for. Sometimes one puncturing object will make quite a lot of holes close together. Try to cover them all with one big patch.

Treating the Cover.

Outwardly, the hole in the rubber should be carefully probed and freed from grit, and then cleaned with gasolene, benzene, or the like solvent. The surfaces of the hole should next be solutioned with two or three coats, and the wound bound up until the solution has set. If the hole gapes, it should be plugged with some of the stopping preparations sold for the purpose. Inwardly, the weak place in the fabric should be reinforced by a piece of prepared canvas extending not only the full width of the cover, but a short distance up the outside as well, so as to be gripped by the rim. This·should be carefully solutioned in place. The canvas should be cleaned with gasolene before applying the coats of solution, plenty of which will be necessary. The cover ought not really to be used for some twelve hours or more, hence the advantage of carrying a spare cover; but if none has been brought, the damaged part should be relieved from strain either by lacing a gaiter round the cover and felloe of the wheel; or, if this cannot be done, a short canvas sleeve may be sewn around the air tube. This sleeve should be large enough to allow the tube to assume its ordinary diameter, but small enough to relieve the cover from strain. Care must be taken not to prick the tube when sewing the sleeve. Actual bursts in the cover must be treated in the same way, but on a larger scale. If a gaiter is employed, it should be laced on while the tire is only lightly inflated. When the inflation is completed, the extra pressure will cause the gaiter to set very closely, as it should do.

Stripping the Wheel.

In case the cover has to be completely detached from the wheel, pull down the bolts near the top of the wheel, and insert two levers, about nine inches apart, under the remaining edge of the cover. Press on the outer ends of the levers, and then push them forward, so that they bridge across the rim, resting on both edges thereof. The edge of the cover at the top of the wheel will now lie on the levers, and may be drawn along them across, and over the edge of, the rim. Pressing down the handles of the levers will assist the operation. When the cover is thus released from the top of the rim, it may be easily withdrawn from the rest thereof.

Before reinstating the tire, the interior of the cover should be liberally dusted with powdered talc, generally called French chalk. Blacklead or grate polish (or, more properly, graphite) forms an efficient, though dirty, substitute for the chalk. All solutioned parts in the cover and on the tube should receive special allowances. Sometimes a quantity of grit and dirt will accumulate in the cover; this may be picked up with a small lump of soft clay or putty.

While the rim is bare, take the opportunity of seeing that it is clean, free from dents and rust, and well covered with enamel. If there are any bare or rusty patches, and it is not convenient to enamel them at the moment, give them a wipe with a greasy cloth, as rust rots canvas quickly. The grease must be cleaned off thoroughly before applying the enamel.

Replacing the Tire.

If the bed of the rim is uneven, see that it is covered with an evenly-laid tight tape. Straighten or replace any security bolts that have got bent, and push them up from the bed. Put a few pumpfuls of air into the inner tube, and place in position in the cover, while the cover is still off the rim. Be very careful to get the valve stem comfortably into the notches in the cover. Turn the wheel round until the valve hole is at the top. Now very carefully place the tire on the upper part of the wheel, so that the further edge goes into the rim, and the valve can be put into its hole without straining to right or left. Work the further edge of the cover into place under the edge of the rim and under the heads of the bolts. Much of this can be done by hand; the levers must be used for the rest.

The parts are now in the position they occupy when the cover has been opened merely, not entirely detached from the wheel. Supposing the air tube has been withdrawn, and is to be replaced, the stem of the valve should be passed into its hole and the valve completed, except for tightening the outside locknut; and the heads of the bolts should be pressed down into the bed of the rim. The tube should be slightly inflated and tucked into the cover, care being taken not to twist it, or to disturb any of the patches. Pass the hand round between the air tube and the rim to make sure that the tube is not caught by any of the bolt heads.

The valve and bolts are next pushed up again, and the other edge of the cover is got back into the rim like the first. The bead may be helped under the edge of the rim by prodding it with the end of the tire lever; but if it is very obstinate it probably means that the air tube has got down between the edges of the cover. If this is suspected, it is much the best to open the tire again, and then reinsert the second edge of the cover, as a nipped tube spells disaster, none the less deadly because deferred. A little judgment is required to pump the air tube tight enough to prevent nipping in this way, and yet not so tight as to prevent the second edge of the cover being got back into place. If the security bolts can be moved up and down in their holes without difficulty, it generally shows that the tube is not being nipped. When satisfied on this point, you may tighten up the nuts of the valve and bolts, and put a little more air into the tire.

The wheel should now be slowly rotated, and the tire pulled and pushed laterally, and pommeled well with the fist. This enourages the parts to assume their proper positions. After a due amount of exercise of this sort, the tire may be fully inflated, and the nuts of the valve and security bolts given a final turn.

Miscellaneous Hints.

After running a few miles, go over these nuts again. It is important to have them tight to prevent the tire creeping or wrenching or blowing off, and to prevent water getting in. Turning corners too fast is a frequent cause of the tires coming off if the bolts are loose; and if the tires are too weak or the speed too high, the cover may split along at the edge of the rim. Under such circumstances a temporary repair may perhaps be made with a gaiter, etc., but a permanent repair is often impossible. Tires stand best when the inflation is kept well up to the mark. If the tire gets flabby it will get pinched between the rim and the ground, will let the water in, will wear out rapidly, will be more likely to sideslip and will waste power.

Cheeseparing does not pay with tires. Have the covers retreaded as soon as they are worn enough to show the first ply of canvas. Do not try to fit the tires of one maker to the rims of another, unless the tire maker approves. Have all difficult repairs done, or completed, as the case may be, by the manufacturers of the tire.

In case a tire is damaged beyond repair, one may remove the air tube and stuff the cover with hay or any other suitable material that may be at hand; or one may lay some thick coils of rope round the rim. But these are expedients only to be resorted to when "in extremis."

If the car is to be put away for any length of time, it is best to jack up all the wheels and to inflate the tires only hard enough to keep them in shape. They should be wiped over occasionally with a rag dipped in warm water, and should be kneaded to maintain their suppleness.

As to solid tires, little advice can be given, except that they should be examined with a view to ascertain that their means of attachment are secure. Any large cuts should be picked out and mended as above described in relation to the covers of pneumatic tires.

Care of a Car on Tour—The man who starts on tour starts with the risk of trouble—unless his outfit is complete, and it is with a view of eliminating all sources of worry that one can lay to one's own charge that the following paragraphs deal with the necessary preliminary preparations to forestall avoidable mischance.

First, says a noted European motorist, the tires should be taken from their wheels, the rims sandpapered inside, and the bed of the rim enameled with some quick-drying enamel. Next the heads of the security bolts should be examined as to their covering. They will generally be found a mass of crumpled leather. Replace with repairing canvas by cutting two pieces to the required shape, snip a small hole in one of the pieces for the stem to pass through, and then press the

solutioned sides together and trim up with scissors. Now rub
the inside of the cover round with a duster, run your hand
round critically for any bits of flint or other puncturing material that may lurk therein, and look for any signs of cracking or chafing in the lining canvas. If you find a suspicious-
looking place, put a patch on, for there is nothing worse for
your tube than an apparently insignificant weakness of the
cover. The tube seems to chafe through at such spots, even
when there is no actual perforation of the cover further than
perhaps one or two layers of the inner canvas. In replacing
the covers use plenty of French chalk, without overdosing,
or you will find it in cakes when you take them off the next
time; chalk your tube, and put a little air in before you get
the last edge of your cover off. Blow them up hard; they stand
a better chance of retaining the air, especially if there are
any patches on the tubes.

Engine Treatment.

Next, you must put your engine in proper trim, and to do
this thoroughly will take both time and patience, to say nothing of a suit of overalls, and, if possible, an inspection pit.
There will no doubt be doors of some sort to the crank-case,
so that you can discover whether there is too much play in
the connecting rod brasses (bushings). Put the particular
crank you are investigating on the bottom dead center, grasp
the connecting rod, and see if you can move it up and down;
if there is any play, say 1/32 inch, the brass had better be
taken up.

It will depend on the position of the inspection door how
you go about this job. If you have one on each side, it will
be easy to get a spanner to the nuts on the big end; drop the
cap and the bottom brass, then push the piston and rod up out
of the way, and pull the top brass out of its seating. Now
place the brasses on the crank pin, hold them together with
thumb and finger, and see how much shake there really is.
Let this be your guide in filing the edges of the brasses, to
do which it is best to lay the smooth file on the bench and

rub the brass to and fro upon it with equal and steady pressure, unless you are an expert hand with the file. Keep trying the brasses on the pin, and reduce each an equal amount as far as possible, until the amount of shake is only just discernible. You may then find it necessary to file something off the cap before reassembling the parts, or you may have to put a piece of tin or zinc under one of the brasses, but whichever commends itself to you, be sure the cap really grips the brasses when the nuts are tightened up, and that there is no space between them. When all is tight, give your engine a turn by hand to see there is no binding. If there is, you have taken too much off the edges of the brasses, and will have to insert a bit of tin, but with reasonable care this should not happen. Then, finding all serene, you go on to the next big end, and repeat the process. These directions do not apply to the usual type of single-cylinder engines, but are applicable to Darracqs.

Valve Treatment.

Valves will now need attention, and for grinding in there are a number of things advertised and recommended. Knife polish and water give good results, assisted by a carpenter's brace with a screwdriver fitted in the chuck. In case of bad pitting, a skim-up in the lathe saves much labor, and when done be sure there is 1/32 inch clearance between the exhaust valve stem and its lifter; if not, make it so. There is no need to get a bearing all over the valve seating. A line of bright contact as wide as a thread is sufficient, but it must go all round the valve. If there is any emery lying about, wash it out with gasolene. It is a good plan to put a piece of waste in the cylinder port while grinding operations are going on. When all the valves are ground in, give the engine another turn round, and see they all have the proper lift. You may find a worn cam and a valve that is opening late and shutting early in consequence.

It would be well at this juncture to ascertain the accuracy of your timing, by turning the engine and checking the relative positions of the exhaust valves and pistons. Where there is a compression cock, push a piece of steel wire, such as a bicycle spoke or a knitting needle, through the orifice, and feel the piston-head as it rises on the exhaust stroke. The valve should shut when the piston is at the highest point. If you have mechanical inlet valves, they should commence to open at the precise moment, or immediately after, the exhaust valves close—that is, when the piston is just at its highest point.

Ignition.

In overhauling the ignition apparatus, it is well to begin at the source of your current, which will most likely be in the form of accumulators or storage cells. Disconnect them from the primary wires, and if they have transparent cases, look at the plates, which should be alternately plum color and grayish blue. See if any particles threaten to bridge the space between positive and negative plates, and if there is much sediment in the bottom. These are both prolific causes of short circuit and untimely failure of your supply of electricity. If all appears well within, test them with a testing lamp of the proper capacity. Four volts two ampères is about the right thing, and if such a lamp burns brightly for several minutes without diminishing in intensity, you can conclude the battery is all right. If you use a voltmeter, it should show over four volts, but under no circumstances use an ammeter, or short the terminals with a file. In one case you will fuse the wiring of the instrument, and in the other you stand a good chance of buckling a plate or loosening some of the paste from which the plates are built up. Before connecting the wires again, see that the terminals are bright and clean, also the ends of the wires; tighten up the nuts with a pair of pliers, and smear with vaseline, or, better still, wrap the lot up in rubber tape. The casual screwdriver or what-not falling across the terminals will then fail to bring about your undoing.

Adjustment of the Coil.

One of the battery wires will lead to the switch, thence to the frame, where it should make a good and sound connection; the other goes to the coil, where it should connect to the primary terminal, generally marked P. The current supplied by this wire now traverses the primary winding of the coil, and comes out at the terminal marked M or T—motor or trembler. The wire from this terminal goes to the contact breaker, and is connected to the blade thereof in the case of a wipe contact, or to the platinum-pointed screw in the case of the make-and-break type. The make-and-break contact will probably require some attention in the shape of filing up or cleaning the platinum rivets on the blade and adjustable screw. Take care when reassembling that the distance between blade and screw is equal in each case—i. e., where there are two or more cylinders—and that the platinums come hard together, backed up by the spring of the blade. Good flat contacts should be filed, or there will be misfiring when you get going.

See that all the blades are the same length; when they are unequal, as is often the case, the cylinders do not all fire in the same relative position of the crank, and loss of power and irregularity in running are the result. The wipe form of contact requires very little attention, but it is well to see that the brass segment is not worn below the fiber, or there will be sparking. The remedy is to turn it up again in the lathe, until the brass is level with the fiber. Now see that your high tension wires are connected properly at the coil, and when satisfied on that point, take out your plugs and lay them on the cylinder cover; connect up, switch on, and turn them on the round by hand until the trembler on the coil buzzes. If there is much sparking, these contacts will have to be filed up and the screw adjusted, to give as high a note as possible without sticking. Switch on and off rapidly, and see the trembler responds every time, and that there is a spark at the plug simultaneously. When you are satisfied on these points, you can replace the plugs and turn your attention to the carbureter.

Examine the Carbureter.

Carbureters are of so many different patterns that it is difficult to prescribe any hard-and-fast rule for dealing with them. Generally speaking, one should examine the float to be certain that the gasolene does not get inside, and if it has been standing some time immersed in the spirit, a shake will determine if it is empty or not; then take out the needle valve and turn on the gasolene. It should flow freely into the float chamber; if not, clean out your supply pipe and gauzes. The jet may be cleared with a strand of copper wire, such as is found in your electrical outfit, or in the case of the Longue-mare type, the spraying cone can be removed and the channels cleared with a penknife. Do not clean them too vigorously, or you may remove some of the metal and cause the spray to deliver too much gasolene. It may be advisable to grind your needle valve with a touch of knife polish, finishing with some pressure but without emery. This should show a bright appearance when the cone of the valve fits the seat, and when the brightness extends all round the valve will be quite tight. In order to keep the valve upright during this process, it is best to put the cover on the float chamber and secure with two or three screws.

The Change Speed Gear.

By moving the gear-changing lever into the several notches of the quadrant, you will see whether the wheels are in line with one another, and should they be otherwise there will no doubt be some form of adjustment by which you can make them so, and perhaps at the same time neutralize to some extent the wear that has taken place on the tooth sides by setting the sliding sleeve further over. This will require some thinking out, as in some cases the speeds are divided up in pairs, and the remedy for one pair will be at the expense of the other.

In case of three-speed gear with direct drive on top speed, the second speed can be set over by deepening the recesses in the positive clutch which locks the divided shaft together, but this is a last resort when the gears are nearly at the end of their tether. The shafts should be tried for wear in the bearings, and, if considerable, the brasses must be taken up in a similar manner as explained for the connecting-rod brasses; or, in the case of plain bushes, they should be renewed.

Look After the Chains, If Any.

Chains should be soaked in kerosene, dried, and immersed in hot tallow. If considerably stretched they should be renewed. It is hopeless to endeavor to remedy a stretched chain by means of the adjusting rod. This is only useful up to a certain point, say to the extent of one link, but after that link has been taken out the difference in pitch between the chain and the sprocket becomes too great for the chain to run properly, and it is forced to ride up the teeth in its endeavor to find its proper pitch circle. At this stage it will save much trouble to invest in a new pair of chains.

Brakes and Bearings.

Give your brakes some attention, and in effecting adjustments be careful to take up equally on each side, or the car will swerve when they are applied, but if you have some compensating device this precaution is unnecessary. The wheels should be separately jacked up, and if showing signs of shake in the bearings should be adjusted, but always leaving just a trifle of play. The axle-caps should be filled with grease before screwing on. By giving the wheel a spin, the presence of a broken ball may be detected, and, if found, removed, and replaced by one of exactly the same size. If it is impossible to procure one which your calipers assure you is the same as the others, it is far better to leave one out than to put in a larger one, though a smaller one would not so much matter. When replacing the gear-box, you should adjust the countershaft brake, and, if necessary, replace the lining of the band.

Attention to Steering Gear.

See that your steering gear is all correct, and if of the direct type be sure the pins on the steering arm, distance rod, and divided axle are securely nutted and pinned. It may not be possible to adjust for wear, but if you have worm and sector or quick pitch thread and nut there should be means of adjustment, in the first case by setting the worm deeper in gear, and in the second by letting up the halves of the nut. In any case, it is very desirable the car should go exactly in the direction you require it, and backlash on the steering gear is irritating, to say the least.

Cleaning out the Water-circulating System.

The water circulation can conveniently be inspected while you are under the car attending to the steering gear, and if you suspect anything faulty, disconnect the several unions, and wash through the radiators, pipes, tanks, and cylinder jackets with the hose and a good force of water. An obstinate block in a pipe will generally yield on the application of heat. Methylated spirit (wood alcohol) on a piece of waste will answer capitally, but the gasolene tank should be empty, or the refractory pipe removed to a safe distance while this operation is going on. The same process may be applied to radiators, with the proviso that you do not carry the heating far enough to melt the solder. The obstruction will generally be found to consist of grease, or some foreign body incased in grease. Boiling water may be applied if you have it handy, and with the addition of washing soda is excellent for tanks. Pour it in hot, and leave for a few hours, and your tank will scale beautifully.

Accessories for the Tour.

If the reader has attended to all the points mentioned in the preceding paragraphs, and has satisfied himself that things are correct, or, if not, has made them so according to the instructions given, he is at last prepared to set out on the projected tour. It now behooves the would-be tourist to collect the necessary impedimenta, which may consist of the following articles:

Spare cover, which may be wrapped in a strip or bag of suitable material; such bags, complete with straps, can be bought of many dealers.

Spare inner tubes—two or more, having regard to the space available.

Repair outfit, with an ample store of solution, patches, and canvas.

A few tire gaiters or tire sleeves. The eyeleted kind require woven steel cable, which is damaging to the fingers, though they can be laced with rawhide thongs instead. These thongs are most useful things to have in your repair kit, as in the event of a burst they can be used as a gaiter by attaching one end to a spoke and winding over the rim and cover in a spiral, and fixing the other end to the next spoke. For this purpose, you will want long ones (6 ft. or so), and they should be applied with the tire deflated; the subsequent inflating pulls them tight on the cover, and if they constrict the part on which they lie, to some extent, so much the better—they will wear all the longer. A tip in putting gaiters and thongs into requisition is to start wrapping some inches behind the burst, when this is in contact with the ground, so as to counteract the creeping tendency.

There are a great many makes of solution on the market—some very good, others indifferent. One "special motor solution" appears to be rubber dissolved in carbon bisulphid, and has an overpowering odor. Some drivers swear by it; much depends on the relative size of the tire to weight of car. The experience of others has been that the rapid evaporation of the solvent produces condensation of atmospheric moisture on the surface of the solution, which prevents the patch sticking. You may be certain that if your car is under-tired there will be constant trouble with patches. Some have found that a canvas patch on the back of the rubber patch, extending an inch or so beyond it all round, helps to keep it on, but nothing short of vulcanization will make a sound job.

Tools, etc., for the Tour.

These may include a strong adjustable wrench; a set of tube spanners; a small vise to fix on mud-guard or step; a hack saw and half a dozen blades; a set of files (one 10-inch flat second cut, one half-round, one square, one round, and a few small warding files); a brace and several sizes of drills, also a screwdriver to fit brace, and one or two center bits for wood; a large screwdriver; two hammers (one heavy, one lighter) ; a lifting jack to suit car axles; links of chain and connecting bolt; a pair of flat-nosed cutting pliers; a small adjustable wrench; a box of assorted nuts, bolts, and split pins; assorted wood screws; copper wire; rubber hose for pump connections; sparking plugs; insulated wire.

Experience will dictate a fairly complete outfit, and, although occupying a good deal of room, such will be worth taking. Having filled the tanks and lubricators, strapped your baggage in the most convenient place, and donned your motoring garments, you set out on your adventurous career.

Stabling of a Car.

At the end of your first day's journey you may elect to spend the night at some village hotel. The chances are that you may not find much accommodation for the car, and here a sheet of waterproof canvas or a properly-made car cover comes in. The latter is provided with cords for fastening down, and is shaped roughly to the vehicle, but a plain sheet 12 ft. square or 12 ft.x14, or 16 ft., according to size of car, will do very well, and only cost half as much. Make fast all round; it will prevent the wind blowing it off, and also tend to preserve any little odds and ends you may have left lying in the tonneau or elsewhere from being annexed, or the lubricator from being turned on by meddlesome people. Before starting in the morning you will gauge your gasolene by dipping a clean stick or rod in the tank, if an indicator is not fitted, and estimate the mileage per gallon used on the previous day. The oil reservoir should be examined, and perhaps by adjusting the carbureter and oil feeds you can obtain better results. As everything has just been tightened up, it is better to err on the generous side for the first day or two as regards lubrication, but if there are indications of overdosing this will easily be seen in looking over the car while running. Half an hour devoted to going over the nuts and bolts which you disturbed in your overhauling will be well spent,

Tire Repairing.

Suppose you experience a curious bumping sensation or hear crackling sounds in the neighborhood of the offside driving wheel, and take a cautious look back to find the tire flat as a pancake. On stopping the car, you will be able to tell by the valve stem if the tire has been down long, for if so it will have assumed a tangential position, owing to the creeping of the inner tube, and then the jack will be requisitioned, as the tube must be taken out bodily for repairs. You will probably put in a spare tube, and after dusting it with a little French chalk, replace the cover, inflate the tire, and drive away. But, on the other hand, you may be able to see the actual offender sticking "in flagrante delicto" from the cover in the shape of a horseshoe nail. Then you will merely remove a couple of feet of cover, fish the tube out, and put a patch on the puncture, not forgetting the extra canvas patch previously mentioned. Look out for nips in replacing the piece of cover. The whole repair is only a matter of minutes, because you have the advantage of knowing the exact location of the trouble.

Leaking Patches.

To take another case of deflation, we will suppose you can find no external evidence of puncture, and knowing the tube to be patched you half suspect one of the patches of having sprung a leak. You attach the tire-pump, and gingerly commence putting some air in; the tire begins to regain its rotundity. So it was only a leaky valve, after all. Vigorous strokes at the pump. Hark! a curious sibilant sound. It's that confounded patch, after all. Your ear will tell you whereabouts the leak is, so only remove as much of the cover as will enable you conveniently to attack the job. You will very likely find that, although the air has burrowed a small channel between the patch and the tube in one place, other portions of the patch are holding on tenaciously. Why they do not stick all over alike is what most owners never can understand. However, while you are wondering, the folks in the tonneau are getting cross, so you must get to work.

Removing Patches.

A drop of gasolene applied with care does wonders in persuading the patch to peel off, and afterwards in cleaning the surface of the tube; but do not apply the solution until you have well roughened the place with glass paper. Put the old patch away for future use, and apply a fresh patch, two coats of solution, spread on thinly and well rubbed in, especially the first (you cannot rub the second coat hard, or the lot peels off), squeeze the patch and tube together as hard as possible with finger and thumb, beginning in the center of the patch and working out to the edges. You may hold a block of wood under the tube and beat the patch with a hammer, if preferred, but go gently. Some men belabor their patches unmercifully, and say they never come off; but judicious beating is generally preferred.

Treating a Burst.

In the case of a burst, it is better to remove the entire cover, if you can spare the time. Clean out the inside with a piece of rag damped with gasolene, and, when dry, fix in a piece of thick canvas which is large enough to go right across and lap over the beaded edge on each side. While this is drying, attend to the tube as previously directed, and after replacing the cover and tube, inflate the tube to a slight degree and apply the tire gaiter. It is quite easy to remove a tire without the aid of a jack by rolling the wheel backward and forward. The procedure is as follows: Remove as much of the bead as you can from the side of the wheel nearest to you, and then take out as much tube as the circumstances will permit; then roll the car forward bodily, and the rest of the cover can be detached and the tube entirely taken out. After taking out the security bolts, with the tire lever you can get the inside bead over the outside lip of the rim as far as the ground, and by rolling the car backward a few feet the cover will be free.

Replacing the Tire.

In putting back the cover, reverse the process, only taking care the valve hole comes right with the places in the tire bead intended for the valve stem to pass through. If, when your first bead is in, you find the valve hole is not opposite the gaps, by rolling the car forward or backward, as the case may be, you can set up a creeping action in the cover that will bring the hole and gap in line. For instance, if the gap is to the right of the hole when you are repairing the right-hand tire, the car must be wheeled forward to effect the purpose. Such a repair as is indicated will not last long, and the cover will have to be vulcanized to be efficiently restored; but supposing you have no spare cover, and do not want to abandon your tour, a fairly good job can be made by any saddler in the town where you stay for the night. Get him to sew a piece of rawhide inside the cover, bringing the stitches through to the outside and herringboning over the gash so as to draw the lips together. If you find the canvas previously put in adheres firmly there is no need to take it out, but sew through the lot. It is a good plan to knot each stitch separately, because in that case if one stitch give it does not loosen the others. The difficulty is to get anyone to take the trouble; the remedy is to do it yourself. When the gash or burst was a large one some drivers have used a tire gaiter inside, first cutting off the eyeleted edges; but this plan has the disadvantage of spoiling a gaiter for outside use. It is well to put another gaiter outside in addition.

Supposing the burst is not of a serious enough character to demand so much reinforcement, you need only stitch another canvas patch over the rawhide, which you have sewn in, to prevent chafing on the edges or threads, and the repair is complete. Properly done, this job will last for hundreds of miles. Of course, if the burst is on or near the tread, the outside gaiter or sleeve must be used to protect the threads from cutting.

More about Tires.

It is a good plan to sink the threads below the surface of the rubber carefully by cutting a slit joining the holes where the thread comes out and goes in at every stitch. Do not cut down into the canvas; you will have to exercise judgment in making the incisions. After making the slit, pull the thread tight, and the loop will disappear below the surface of the tire. The thread is now protected, and has also got a better hold of the canvas.

If you are a real enthusiast there will always be plenty to do in the evening after you have dined—little adjustments of the running gear, and perhaps tire repairs—and provided with an electric lamp you can continue your labors after dark, so as to waste no time in the morning. Washing down should always be done under your own inspection, or when next you essay to start away the carbureter will be found full of water or the tremblers submerged. Before applying the hose, look round the tires, see that the wing nuts are tight, and stop any small cuts in the cover with some stopping material. If wet gets inside it will surely cause trouble. See the car thoroughly dried before it is put away for the night. Steering joints are apt to rust up unless protected with coverings. The latter should be fitted to every car, as they are easy to make, and save no end of bother and fatigue from stiff steering.

Misfiring.

The chief complaint from which engines suffer is the fault of missing fire. A fruitful cause of irregular ignition is weakness of the accumulator, so when it occurs you will begin at that end of the electrical gear and satisfy yourself that all is well with the battery. Next have a look at the other end—the plugs—and then go over the ground between. Are the contact blades rubbing firmly on the cam? Are the tremblers on the coil vibrating angrily? You will find out by opening the compression cocks and turning the engine slowly. Suppose one trembler is only fluttering. You remove the contact screw and find it badly pitted. The rivet on the blade has a minute point fused on it, just opposite the part of the screw that has become pitted. A few strokes of a smooth file, a little adjustment of the contact screw, and you are rewarded with a buzz that can be heard some distance away. It may be a high-tension wire that has touched the exhaust pipe and lost its insulation, or a low-tension wire that has chafed against a water pipe, or a loose terminal on the contact breaker. Sometimes the earth return wire gets broken where it is fastened to engine or frame, and then the misfiring will occur intermittently, first in one cylinder and then in the other, leading you a pretty dance until you stumble on the cause. A wipe contact should have ample means of return. The film of oil on the bearings of the second speed shaft and the other resistances between the little brass inset and the frame of the car are almost certain to interfere with a free return, so it is better to provide some other means of return, such as a wire attached to the plate on which the blades are mounted and connected to a nut on the engine or frame. A good plan is to fix a supplementary blade to rub on the center of the fiber cam so as to make contact on the shaft on which the cam is fixed, and ground the wire from this blade.

Examine the Carbureter.

If you are sure the ignition is all right and the missing still persists, suspect the carbureter. A partly blocked gasolene pipe will produce the symptoms, so remove the nut which connects the gasolene pipe. with carbureter, and try blowing back into the tank with the tire pump. This is the rough and ready method. If it fails, disconnect the pipe altogether, and see if it is clear. The pump will clear it if you can make a joint of some sort, either by removing the valve connection or using a bit of rubber tube, or even wrapping a piece of rubber strip round and wiring it in place. The obstruction may be in the narrow orifice below the needle valve; you can find out by dismantling the carbureter. There may be a particle of dirt in the spray nozzle, which gets carried up occasionally to the tiny hole that delivers the gasolene jet, and occasionally drops back to the bottom of the passage. Clean the jet out thoroughly and wash through the passages with gasolene, when no further trouble should be experienced on the road.

PART X.

LAYING UP A CAR.

Laying Up a Car—When a car is to be laid up for any length of time care should be taken to see that it is first properly prepared by a special course of treatment.

The first care should be to see that the engine is thoroughly cleaned in the manner prescribed under Care and Maintenance, in one of the preceding chapters. Any repairs and adjustments that appear necessary can profitably be made at this time so that the car will come out in good shape after its period of rest or storage. Always remember that one cannot expect a car to come out in good running order unless it is in fit condition when laid away.

Transmission Gear.

The change speed gear should be washed out with kerosene in a similar manner to the engine. If the car is a direct driven one, the bevel gear case should be filled with grease, there being no necessity to clear this out, though it would do no harm if it were washed out with kerosene and fresh grease put in. The change speed gear box lid should be removed, or probably in many instances it would be better to remove the top half of the gear box completely so as to expose the gear wheels contained therein, for inspection purposes. The gear-shafts should be felt for slackness, and if any motion except a slight movement endwise is noticed, they had better be seen to at once by the repair man. If the gears are found to be in good order and require no attention, the gear-box should be filled up to the under side of the gearshaft with gear-box oil or lubricating oil and grease, about one-third of the latter to two-thirds of the former.

Connections and Chains.

All the pins, joints, and connections should be well oiled; in fact, it would be better to remove these, cleaning them thoroughly and replacing them, having previously given them a good coating of vaseline. The wheels should be jacked up and removed from their axles, these and the axle-boxes being cleaned out and well greased before replacing. When going round the car, attention should be given to the anchored ends of the springs, and the shackles on the free ends of these should also be well greased. These are some of the points which are particularly liable to be overlooked when going through the process of overhauling and cleaning. Where chain drive is employed, the chains should be removed from the sprockets and well cleaned in kerosene, after which they should be immersed in melted tallow and allowed to remain in this for several hours. Remove the chains, and hang them up to allow the superfluous grease to drain off.

The Clutch.

Special attention should be given to the clutch. This should be withdrawn as far as possible, and its surface well cleaned with gasolene, after which it should be given a good coating of neatsfoot or castor oil. Some have used successfully a mixture of one-half castor oil to one-half of glycerine. It is well to note that the application of clutch dressings is useless unless the clutch leather, where used, is in a condition to absorb some portion of the dressing applied. Thus it happens that a slipping clutch will soon attain so hard a surface that it cannot take up any of the moisture it needs so badly when any dressing is applied. An application of gasolene—assisted by a hard brush—will bring the clutch leather to a state in which it may be successfully treated. Look to the adjustment that it does not slip or grip too tightly. If the clutch be interconnected with the side brakes, pay particular attention to the adjustment here, as it requires very careful checking to act properly.

The Protection of Exposed Metallic Parts.

After having attended to the engine and gearing, the next thing is carefully to go over all the metallic parts of the frame and of the connecting rods used in conjunction with the steering gear, change speed gear, and the brakes. Where the paint has been scratched or barked sufficiently to expose the metal, this should be rubbed bright with a piece of emery cloth, and paint or air-drying enamel applied, giving it at least two coats of either. All plated or polished parts should be given a coating of pure vaseline after they have been thoroughly cleaned and polished. Pure vaseline, as obtained from the druggist, is specified as distinct from the commercial article, which is not so pure, containing as it does salts which are injurious to nickel or silver-plated parts, whereas the refined vaseline has no effect upon them. In the course of a few runs the greased bright parts will collect a certain amount of dirt, which, if necessary, should be very carefully removed with a piece of rag soaked in kerosene. The dirt should be scraped rather than rubbed off, as the rubbing is liable to cause scratches. A long, slow sweeping stroke of the kerosene rag takes up the dirt without using it as an abrasive material. This is a very important point, for scratched brass or plated work looks extremely bad. If the mud of many months be allowed to accumulate over the vaseline, it will do no harm, for it bears the same relation to the grease surfaces as the hair of a rabbit skin; you cannot remove the one without the other.

Lubricators.

All the lubricators should be drained of any oil which they may contain, and should be thoroughly washed out with kerosene or stale gasolene. Where sight-feed lubricators are fitted, or types which necessitate the using of lengths of copper pipe to convey the lubricant from its receptacle to the bearings, such pipes should be removed, and should have kerosene passed through them. For this purpose, a syringe is the best instrument to use, as the cleansing fluid can be passed through the tubes at a pressure which will insure any obstruction caused by the congealing of the oil, or by other causes, being swept away. If this is done and the pipes are reconnected, when the car is taken out again one will know that all that is necessary for good working of those parts is a fresh supply of lubricating oil.

Tire Treatment.

We now come to the question of tire treatment, and here it is somewhat difficult to advise, for there are variations in each and every make of tire. That is to say, there are some tires of one make which wear very much better than others, and these are always worth retreading if the fabric is good; others there are in which slices of rubber come away from the fabric wholesale, leaving it to be attacked by wet, and thereby ruining it for retreading purposes. The question as to when a tire needs repairing is one of sympathetic judgment. We have seen men cheerfully running tires upon whose treads there was scarcely an ounce of rubber left, and yet they talked of having them retreaded "when the rubber was all gone." Directly a bad cut in the rubber is observed, a rule should be made of having it attended to at the first opportunity. The cut should be washed out with water to remove dirt, and then carefully dried. Gasolene should then be wiped or brushed into the cut to further clean the surfaces and prepare them for the coating of rubber solution, which should be next applied. After the solution has been left for about ten minutes or a little more, the cut may be filled up with one of the many preparations which are now sold for the purpose. Failure in a repair is invariably traceable to insufficient cleansing or experimental treatment. Any cuts which are found in the covers should be dealt with on the lines indicated above. If one has any suspicion that any particular tire is in such condition that it may at any time become a "lame duck," have it off; it saves hours (possibly on the roadside) at a later date. This is also a good opportunity to repair any punctured inner tubes which may be on hand. For this purpose there are handy vulcanizers to be obtained if one wishes to do the work oneself.

Laying up for the Winter.

Having now indicated the general lines of treatment to pursue in preparing a car for winter use, we must consider the owner who, for special reasons, is compelled to lay up his car during the whole of the winter. The car to be laid up should be treated on the general lines already laid down, but some further attention is also necessary. When the car is brought in after its final run, the first thing to be done is to remove the cushions, aprons, lamps, horn, and all the tools and spare parts. The battery should be taken from its box, and it would be advisable to remove the coil and all the wires connected with the electrical ignition apparatus. When doing this, a rough sketch should be made showing the method of wiring, as when these parts have to be replaced it is as well to have a definite guide at hand, for in the interval between the putting away and bringing out the car it is the easiest thing in the world to forget the terminals to which particular wires should be connected.

Care of the Engine.

As to the engine, some additional attention is needed, particularly with regard to the interior of the cylinders. These should be well washed out with kerosene followed by a little gasolene. This treatment dissolves any oil which may be on the cylinder walls or piston, and which may cause them to stick, and it prevents the oxidation of the oil if it is allowed to remain. As to painting the engine over, which is often advisable, some owners inquire if it will be necessary to clean off the paint before running the engine again, and if so, they strongly object to following this course. It would of course, be necessary to remove the protecting coating, otherwise when the engine began to get warm with running the paint would make itself particularly disagreeable. There is not much difficulty in removing such a covering if olive oil be used, as the olive oil never sets hard, and is therefore readily attacked by turpentine or gasolene. If the engine is not so covered, it may present a lamentable spectacle after a few weeks' standing. If not painted the engine should receive a coating of vaseline. Particular attention should be paid to the exposed portions of the valve stems, as should they become at all rusty, they are liable to stick in their guides and cause trouble. These should in any case be well coated with vaseline. As to the remainder of the car, it should be treated on the lines already laid down, with one or two exceptions, which we will proceed to deal with.

Battery Treatment.

The battery, when battery ignition is used, forms the principal object for attention among those parts which have been removed from a car, and great care will have to be taken with this for its proper preservation. It should be tested, and if found to be below its full voltage it should be recharged until this voltage is attained. The acid should now be poured out from the cells of a wet battery, which should be washed out with clean rain water two or three times so as to remove all the acid, and they should afterwards be filled up with pure clean rain water to a point the height of a quarter of an inch above the top of the plates. The rubber stoppers should now be replaced. While washing out the cells, the terminals also should be carefully washed to free them from all traces of acid. They should be wiped dry, and given a coat of pure vaseline as a further protection against their corrosion.

As many cells are filled with a semi-solid electrolyte, it is impossible to subject such to the above treatment, and as the acid cannot be removed from the cell, there is only one course of satisfactory treatment open, and that is to have the batteries recharged every six weeks at least. In the meantime, a small four-volt lamp should be connected in the circuit, and should occasionally be allowed to remain lighted for a period of, say, half an hour, so as to enable the battery to discharge itself to a slight extent. This helps to keep the plates in much better order than the mere recharging at stated intervals without any discharge having taken place.

Dry batteries can be dismissed in a few words. As nothing can be done to assist them in retaining their energy, it is as well to take advantage, if possible, of what current they are still capable of giving off. The cells may be used to energize electric bells, or they may be used for a glow lamp or some such purpose.

The Coil.

The induction coil requires but little attention. It should be put away in a dry place, and out of all danger of being subjected to high temperatures. For instance, it should not be put in a cupboard against that side of the wall where the chimney is likely to give off more than a medium temperature. It will thus be seen that the only requirements are to protect the coil from damp and from excessive heat. The reason for this is that paraffin wax is often used as an insulating material, and if this substance becomes sufficiently heated to melt, in many coils the insulation would be entirely broken down, on account of there not being sufficient non-conducting material on the wires. So that if this were to happen such coils would be absolutely ruined. Obviously, therefore, cold, so long as the atmosphere is dry, does not injuriously affect the coil.

Laying up Tires.

The tires need very special attention. They should be removed from the wheels, the air tubes carefully examined and tested, and if found to be in good condition they should be treated with a liberal supply of French chalk, and put into a bag or box, and stowed away, preferably in a dark room where an even medium temperature obtains. The covers themselves should be very carefully examined, and all cuts, whether large or small, should be treated in the manner already described. If this is not to the liking or beyond the capabilities of the owner, the tires might be sent to the manufacturers for general overhauling and repairs. This would really be the most satisfactory procedure. For the storage of the outer covers of the tires, the same conditions apply to the inner tubes. As their bulk is much greater than that of the inner tubes, the most handy method of protecting them for storage is to bandage them round with strips of canvas. An owner once had occasion to lay by a set of motor car tires, and instead of using French chalk for the outer covers, he used flowers of sulphur in a very liberal manner. After the tires had lain by for some four months or so, they were brought out, and looked as fresh and as good as ever. Not only so, but they showed no signs whatever of hardening or cracking, and retained their elasticity to the fullest degree. This was probably due to the fact that sulphur is the principal component used in the vulcanization of indiarubber. It is noticeable, as a general rule, that in the course of time the sulphur exudes from the rubber, leaving it in a very spongy form, thus allowing air to enter. This hardens the material, so that it eventually breaks up into small patches. The owner aforesaid tried the sulphur, therefore, as a matter of experiment, on the theory that sulphur thus applied to the outside of the covers would prevent that which was contained in the substance of the rubber itself from working out. He was pleased to note that his theory was borne out by practice. If it is not convenient to remove the tires from the wheels, the car should be jacked up and packing put underneath the axles, so that the wheels may be kept well off the ground.

Lamps.

Lamps, whether of the oil or acetylene type, should be thoroughly well cleaned and polished, wrapped in cloths, and stored in a dry place. Particular care should be taken to cleanse thoroughly the carbide container of acetylene lamps of all deposit, and to dry the interior of the vessel carefully before putting it away. If any carbide is allowed to remain in the container for any length of time it will form such a hard and solid mass as to endanger the container when it is removed by forcible means at a later stage. All oil and wicks should be removed from the vessels of oil lamps, and as a further precaution against the action of stale oil at a later period, they may be washed with a strong solution of hot soda and water, afterwards being carefully wiped out, or if a cloth cannot be inserted into the oil well, they should be dried by evaporation.

The horn which should have been removed at the same time as the aforementioned parts, should be cleaned and put away with the lamps.

A Covering for the Car.

Having now taken all the needful precautions for the protection of the car in detail, we next have to consider the vehicle as a whole. Even in the very best of garages, it is well to cover the whole of the vehicle, including the bonnet, with a light sheet, the edges of which are provided with tapes to enable it to be tied down into position over the car. Such vehicles as are provided with hoods or canopies present some little difficulty in this way, owing to the immense size of sheet which would be required to cover the car as a whole. Except for the really efficient protection of such cars as are so fitted, two sheets would be necessary, one of which would cover the body completely, slots being. cut in the edges of this sheet at suitable points, so that the rods supporting the canopy would not interfere with the complete protection of the carriage body. If it is thought absolutely necessary to protect the canopy by reason of its being fitted with expensive curtains, a second sheet should be thrown over this, allowing it to hang down to a sufficient extent to meet the sheet which is placed over the car. Leather hoods should not be allowed to remain for any long period in a folded-up position, for however good the leather may be, and whatever means are taken to provide for its protection and the retention of its suppleness, it will dry and crack where sharp bends occur in it. For this reason it is well, if possible, to let the hood remain open during such time as the car is standing in the garage.

PART XI.

GASOLENE—ITS PROPERTIES AND ECONOMICAL USE.

Economy in consumption of fuel in any kind of engine consists in using just enough fuel for the purpose, and also, where the fuel is a combination of different elements, in using these elements combined in the cheapest way where one is of higher value than the other. It will pay the motorist to study out the proper proportions of gasolene to air. A great deal more air is required than gasolene. It has been found that a gas mixture in which there is too much gasolene not only reduces the power of the engine, but sets up internal troubles due to sooting up and overheating, so that if the proportion of air is too small, an extravagant proportion of the substance which has to be purchased is perforce being employed, and at the same time the engine efficiency is decreased and its mechanism injured.

This shows that the great and most important point as regards economy in consumption of gasolene is the proper designing and functioning of the carbureter. At present, fortunately, the manufacturers' attention is being drawn to correct design so as to obtain always a constant mixture, and also a mixture as efficient as possible. Generally speaking, the driver errs on the side of giving too much gasolene rather than too much air.

Another consideration is the speed of the engine. An engine will give out its greatest efficiency, that is to say, the heat units of fuel consumed will be least in proportion to the work done when the engine is running at the speed at which it was designed to run. If it runs faster than this, it will be extravagant; if it runs slower it will require a richer mixture, and, therefore, a larger proportion of gasolene to air, and so in this instance also economical methods are not achieved. It is, therefore, advisable to run the engine as nearly as possible at a constant speed. In the case of an internal combustion engine as used on motor vehicles, however, this is practically impossible, but is approximated by means of the change speed gear.

The greatest economy in fuel can only be obtained by very careful driving and a thorough understanding of what is going on in the engine under varying circumstances. For this reason the reader should refer to the article on Driving, in which the manipulation of the control levers as regards air and throttle—in order to secure efficiency—is fully dealt with. He must bear in mind that the best results as regards speed and power obtained, and reduction in wear and tear of engine, will be achieved by practising economy; in other words, if he tries to force the engine by giving it a rich charge, he will not only fail to obtain the required result, but overheating, carbonizing, knocking, preignition, and many other troubles will soon make their presence evident.

Economy of gasolene, as it is generally understood by the automobilist, refers to economy in covering a certain distance. It is for this reason that in reliability trials the gasolene consumption is reckoned in ton miles, the speed being considered fairly constant for the car—that is, a speed of something about twenty miles per hour. Of course, the automobilist who averages over this speed will find that the consumption increases because the wind resistance, and, therefore, the power required to propel the vehicle on an even surface, increases as the square of the velocity.

This ton mileage method of arriving at economy also leaves out of consideration the nature of the roads and other resistances offered to the movement of the car, so that the economy will be affected adversely if excessively bad roads or heavy head winds are met with, or if the speed is high.

This method of regarding the subject precludes the fact that all these conditions make the engine do more work. Thus, if the engine is to be run economically, the driver must look to what is taking place in the engine and car itself. It is obvious that he cannot level out hills or smooth out roads or prevent head winds; it is also obvious that he can make the work which is actually done in the engine and car itself as small as possible, so that it is clear that economy will be affected if the engine is not in thorough working order.

Loss of compression will affect the power of the engine, but at the same time the engine will be using as much fuel, the result being that it will not propel the car the same distance, or against the same resistance, as it would if it were in proper working order, and thus economy in actual results is lost. In the same way the transmission mechanism (which includes the whole of the construction of the car which transmits the power from the engine to the road wheels), if it is not in proper order, will affect economy because it will absorb power, so that to perform the same amount of work as regards moving the car the engine will have to use more fuel.

The quality of the fuel used also bears on the question, although nowadays, with improved carbureters and a more uniform standard of specific gravity for gasolene, the condition of the fuel does not count for so much as it did in the old days. Another considerable loss of economy arises if the gas charge is not ignited and expanded at the proper moment; that is to say, the full length of the working stroke of the piston should be taken advantage of. It is obvious that if ignition of the gas charge is delayed until after the piston has commenced to descend on what should be the power stroke, a great deal of its efficiency will be lost as regards the pressure exerted on the piston.

When the density of gasolene has reached a point which interferes with its free evaporation it is called "stale" gasolene. It then makes an imperfect mixture for motor-car engines, but is useful for removing grease and dirt from metal parts of the car.

Gasolene is a light, volatile, colorless liquid commonly obtained by the distillation of petroleum and forming one of the series of hydrocarbons for motor cars. Much used as a fuel in internal combustion engines. Motor spirit is usually called "Petrol" in the British Isles, "Essence" in France (short for "Essence de pétrole"), "Benzin" in Germany, "Benzina" in Italy, etc.

When the crude petroleum, as drawn from the wells, is placed in a closed vessel and heated, the most volatile parts evaporate first. This vapor is caught and cooled (the combination of the boiler and condensing apparatus constitute a still), and the liquids which settle in the condenser come over, and have a specific gravity varying from 0.629 to 0.667 in the case of gasolene; to 0.802 for kerosene, and 0.875 for lubricating oils. Other petroleum products include cymogene, sp. gr. 0.588, naphtha, benzine, etc.

Gasolene is the first distillation before kerosene, that is, gasolene is a mixture of petroleum ether and benzoline. Chemically speaking, it consists to the extent of 75 per cent, or more, of methanes with some heptanes. The remainder is ethenes with traces of benzines.

Benzine is the unfortunate commercial name given to "A" naphtha, which tends to confusion with another substance which is a coal-tar product.

In ordering gasolene in Europe the scale often used for indicating the density is that of Beaumé. Zero on this scale corresponds to the density of a solution of salt of specified proportions, and ten degrees corresponds to the density of distilled water at a specified temperature or to a specific gravity of unity. The portion of the stem of the instrument lying between these two points is divided into ten equal parts, and the rest of the stem is divided into divisions of equal size up to ninety degrees. Higher numbers indicate lower specific gravities—a rather confused arrangement.

The actual instrument used is a densimeter or hydrometer.

The specific gravity of what is sometimes called .680 gasolene varies with temperature, but is supposed to be measured at 60°Fahrenheit. It is .667 at 87°F., and .693 at the freezing point, 32°F.

Vaporization Experiments—The vaporization of gasolene requires a surface per H.P. of 221 square centimeters, heated to about 82° C., the pressure of the vapor mixture being 760 millimeters of mercury. The gasolene must fall on the surface drop by drop. In the case of spraying carbureters, the velocity of the air must be 25 meters per second; the vaporization surface can thus be less than 221 square centimeters. The vapor diffuses in air with a velocity of 5 millimeters per second. Knowing the speed of the suction, it is easy to calculate the openings in the gauze required and the length of suction pipe in order that the gasolene vapor may have time to completely penetrate the air before it is admitted to the cylinder. The vaporization of kerosene requires a surface of 200 square centimeters per H.P. heated to a temperature of 220° C., the pressure being 760 millimeters of mercury.

GASOLENE HINTS AND TIPS.

A Cheap Gasolene Gauge.

A very efficient and cheap form of gasolene gauge can be fashioned from a sufficient length of ground-glass rod, which should be fairly stout. Run your car on to a level place, empty your tank and then measure the gasolene back therein, gallon by gallon. After the introduction of each gallon sound the tank with the ground-glass rod and the height of the spirit therein will be plainly visible on the rod. Mark the height of each successive gallon on the rod with the edge of a sharp file, and, the rod being kept in a leather clip handy to the tank, you will have a ready means of determining how much gasolene there remains in your tank at any time.

Gasolene Leaks.

One often hears of abnormal gasolene consumption in certain cars, while sister cars are known to run far more economically, and this is put down as a rule to the driver. To a great extent the gasolene consumption is under the control of the driver, but very often slight leaks in the gasolene system are responsible for a considerable amount of gasolene being wasted, and as the gasolene evaporates immediately, it is exposed to the air, these leaks escape notice, and the owner's pocket suffers accordingly. If a high consumption is experienced, and the ordinary remedies fail, we would suggest using a mixture of gasolene and kerosene, say, in proportions of one gallon of kerosene to four gallons of gasolene, when the kerosene will percolate through any leaks, but will not evaporate, thus rendering the locality of the leak easy to determine. As soon as the leaks are found out and repaired gasolene alone can be used again if desired. An alternative is to place in the gasolene tank a few grains of some aniline dye. This will color the gasolene, say, a dark blue, without affecting its qualities. The dyed gasolene will now pass through these leaks and leave a stain wherever a leak occurs.

It is a good plan to carry a length of rubber piping which nicely fits on the gasolene pipe from the tank to the carbureter. If the tank should ever leak seriously that rubber pipe can be put on one end on to the gasolene pipe. The other end, which has a short length of metal pipe, will be put through the cork of one of the two two-gallon cans of gasolene which should be always carried in the car, irrespective of what may be in the running tank, and by propping or holding up this can the driver will be able to get gasolene to the carbureter, and reach home or a place where the tank or its connections can be repaired.

Gasolene Supply.

When touring in remote districts, where gasolene supplies are infrequent, and where the quality is of a doubtful character, one naturally wishes to carry as large a supply of satisfactory spirit as possible. The storing of this, however, in two-gallon cans is inconvenient in many instances, as, no matter how neatly they are packed when starting out, they are

Knox Model "O" Transmission Gears, Shafts and Bearings.

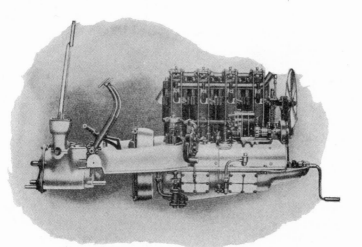

Knox Model "O" Power Plant—Water Cooled.

certain sooner or later to become dislodged, either for the purpose of removing baggage or obtaining spare parts, tools, etc., and they are never repacked as neatly as they were before. Even if they retain their original position, there is always the fear of their becoming upset through the vibration of the car when traveling. In many types of motor vehicles there is ample room for the placing of a tank in which may be carried any quantity of gasolene up to, say, twenty or thirty gallons. Generally these tanks should be located beneath the floorboards of the car, having a convenient filling cap on the outside of the car, or by lifting a floorboard in the back seats of the car. The cap should be perfectly airtight, and provided with an air pressure valve and permanent connections to the ordinary gasolene tank. When it is desired to replenish the latter, it would only be necessary to turn on the tap between the spare tank and the regular supply tank. Then, by means of the tire pump, sufficient pressure is raised in the spare tank to force the spirit from that into the second receptacle— an obviously easier and cleaner procedure than the unscrewing and filling up from cans, to say nothing of less waste, as the spare tank could be filled at a quicker rate than the ordinary tank. In addition to being much safer, this arrangement gives much more space for baggage, not to mention the passengers' feet and limbs.

For Straining Gasolene.

A Boston, Mass., automobilist contributes a good tip for the straining of gasolene before putting it into the tank. He says: "I have found the best quality (jewelers') chamois skin makes a most excellent medium for straining gasolene. It stops dirt, fluff and water, so far as my experience shows, and if the opening of the funnel is 8 inches in diameter, so that a good-sized piece of skin may be used, it does not materially delay the filling of the tank."

It is often a somewhat difficult matter to get car owners to realize the necessity for straining gasolene as it is poured into the supply tank of the car. Even men who have owned cars for some time neglect this important though apparently small matter. They invariably start off by straining their gasolene, but sometimes when the strainer is not at hand they simply pour the contents into the supply tank from the can direct. Because nothing has happened they have continued this practice, with the result that they have got an accumulation of dirt which sooner or later reaches the carbureter, causing a great deal of trouble and annoyance before it is finally got rid of. Rather than fill up the tank with unstrained gasolene, it is better to use a pocket handkerchief folded twice or three times, or even four times, according to the texture of the material, and make a strainer of it. Of course, the handkerchief, after being employed in this way, is not desirable for personal use.

An Improved Gasolene Filter.

Another owner writes: "It has been my experience that gasolene is continually getting dirtier, and only during the past year or so have I had to clear my gasolene supply pipes on account of sluggish running, and I am (or rather was) surprised to find so much dirt. It occurred to me that a more efficient filter could be easily made to filter the spirit so perfectly that no solid matter or sediment could ever get into the tank. The following was adopted, and the arrangement has proven most satisfactory:

"Take an ordinary funnel, and remove (by melting the solder) the lower end. Buy a pepper dredger, knock the bottom out, and after straightening and cleaning the edges, solder this on to the top part of the original funnel.

"Enlarge by drilling small holes in the copper lid of the pepper-box, and your filter is complete when a small circular piece of linen is placed under the cover of the pepper-box. A supply of linen disks should be kept, for I find that a new one is required for filtering each can of gasolene."

Auxiliary Gasolene Tank for Touring Purposes.

Where gravity feed is used for the gasolene supply to the carbureter, the gasolene tank is often fitted as high as possible under the driver's seat, this giving just about sufficient head of gasolene to allow of satisfactory working on ordinary give-and-take roads. However, when touring through hilly districts, it is found that at times there is difficulty in maintaining the proper gasolene feed to the carbureter, so that just at the time when most gasolene is needed less is obtained. To get over this difficulty, a spare tank can be fitted at the forward end of the car, and connected to the carbureter, so that the fact of having hill-climbing to do would allow of really a higher head of gasolene to be supplied to the carbureter, so that no difficulty in climbing the worst of hills can be caused by failure of the gasolene supply to the carbureter.

On Repairing Gasolene Tanks.

Should a tank or other vessel which has contained gasolene require repairs calling for a soldering iron, great care should be taken to clear such tank of any gasolene fumes which may remain therein, otherwise there is the possibility of an explosion occurring. Gasolene fumes being heavier than air will remain in any vessel for a considerable time, even though it has an opening to the air. There are several ways of clearing away such fumes, of which turning the tank with its opening to the lowest point and leaving it so for several hours is the easiest. Another method is to subject the tank to indirect heat in a similar position to that mentioned; that is, perhaps, the quickest method, though not always convenient. In any case, it is always advisable to keep it, if a blow lamp is used, as far away from the tank as possible.

Fitting a Float to a Tank.

Every driver feels the need of a float for showing the height of the gasolene in the tank, though only the most modern cars are so fitted. We show a simple method of fitting a float to any tank without cutting the tank open. The ordinary filling cap A is removed, and centrally in it is made a hole. Through this hole is passed a nipple B, which is soldered in place. The nipple is formed with a shoulder providing suitable holding surface for the solder in spite of the usual thinness of the filling cap. Through this nipple B is passed a wire C attached to a float D. Replacing the filling cap, the float will rise, and the wire passing through the nipple will indicate how much fuel there is in the tank. Generally speaking, it is advisable to make the float to withdraw from the tank with the filling cap. For this purpose the end of the wire can be riveted over, or provided with a ball, as shown at E. On the top of the nipple is screwed a cap F, which normally keeps the

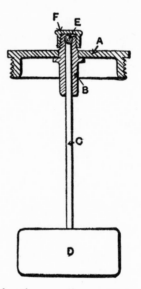

float down. Directly the small cap F is removed, the float will rise. Of course, the float D is made sufficiently small to pass through the ordinary filling opening, and care must be taken not to damage the float when the cap A is removed. In making a float suitable for the purpose, it is advisable to test its buoyancy in gasolene, after the wire C has been fixed. A float which is sufficiently buoyant in water is nothing like so buoyant in gasolene, and much time can be saved by first testing this point.

PART XIII.

OPERATING MECHANISM.

The control mechanism of a typical modern (1909) automobile is described below:

Steering Wheel—The wheel is constructed of bronze with hard rubber grip. This is a special feature; the wheel is a very strong and the grip is unaffected by the weather and always presents a neat and attractive appearance.

Steering Gears—The power exerted through the wheel is communicated to the steering gears—the worm and sector— which are of special steel. The parts are thoroughly lubricated and completely protected.

Steering Mechanism—A short vertical shaft connects the sector with the steering connecting rod, its upper end fitting over a hexagon taper on the sector and locked with a castellated nut, and the lower end is ball shaped, forming part of the universal joint at the rear end of the steering connecting rod. Buffer springs are placed at both ends of the steering connecting rod to absorb the shock caused by jolting over rough roads; hexagon nuts hold the springs and socket joints in place, these nuts being pinned in place so nothing can work loose, and yet when desired may be removed for the purpose of thoroughly cleaning all the parts; the universal joints at both ends of the steering connecting rod are packed in grease and protected by leather boots. The front tie rod is placed back of the front axle.

Spark Lever—Placed on top of steering wheel and stamped "Spark." When pulled back toward the operator as far as it will go the spark is fully retarded and when pushed as far forward on the quadrant as it will go the spark is fully advanced.

Hand Throttle—A small lever stamped "Gas" is placed on top of the steering wheel and as it is pushed forward the throttle is opened. The throttle is of the balanced type and operated by the governor, and the adjustment is such that when the hand throttle on the wheel is fully opened the governor will prevent the motor from racing.

Foot Throttle—This is a pedal operated by the right foot; when fully depressed it opens the throttle wide and overcomes the action of the governor.

Gear Shift Lever—This is placed so as to be operated conveniently by the right hand. The various positions of the lever give the following results: Outer Quadrant: lever farthest forward,—Reverse; next position back,—First Speed; central position,—Neutral; rear position,—Second Speed. Inner Quadrant: front position,—Third Speed; central position,—Neutral; rear position,—Fourth Speed.

Brake Lever—This is a hand lever placed just beyond the gear shift lever; the brakes are engaged by pulling the lever back.

PART XIV.

CHOICE OF A CAR, ETC.

To the average man the purchase of an automobile usually involves many important considerations, including those of price, cost of upkeep and adaptability for the buyer's purpose.

The question of choice among the numerous makes and models of cars now offered to the public may be considered under two general heads, namely, in relation to new cars purchased from the makers or an agent and second-hand cars bought from a private owner or a dealer.

"In choosing a car," writes an autoist who has been through the mill, "one has a good many things to consider. First, perhaps, comes the sadly sordid question of cost, and this question has several subsidiary ones tacked on to it. Are you prepared to spend enough to buy a thoroughly sound car of well-known make, and are you prepared to devote a proper amount to its upkeep? Do you realize that a certain annual expenditure above and beyond gasolene, etc., is necessary to a motor car? Or are you only disposed to lay out the price of a good second-hand car? Do the claims of gasolene, of steam, or of electricity appeal most strongly to you? How many passengers do you desire to accommodate, and what horse-power will you consider necessary? Will you be content with low power which will propel you at decent speed on the level, but will require the lower speeds for hill work, or would you prefer sufficient engine power to carry you up gradients of 1 in 10 without changing down? Do you propose to do your own driving, or is your automobiling to be of so strictly amateur a character that you will keep a chauffeur who will do all the driving? You say your friend has a So-and-so that never gives him any trouble, and you mean to have the same? Well, there is something in that, provided your friend's requirements and accomplishments are the same as your own; but not necessarily otherwise. Perhaps he will sell you his car. There is nothing like knowing the antecedents of a second-hand investment."

There is a widespread opinion that every beginner should learn on a small car of moderate horse-power. He will learn quicker than on a big car, and in the trying days of his novitiate will be less likely to prove a danger to himself and the general public. There is an absence of responsibility about a modest light car, and the driver gains confidence rapidly, whereas the big car proves a constant strain to his nerves. His mistakes, too, prove far less expensive. With a big expensive car ignorance or carelessness may cost him considerable money within the first few months. With a small car he is less likely to make mistakes that cause damage, while the cost of making good such damage as may occur is trifling as compared with the big car. From the pleasure point of view he will derive just as much value from a light car as if he aspired higher before gaining experience, and will at the same time have in reserve the keen pleasure of graduating on to smoother running vehicles of greater horse-power, until the limit which he can afford has been reached. Even when he has attained the summit of his ambition he will still possess a kindly affection for the small light car, and will find it advantageous from an economical, pleasurable, and convenience point of view to keep one in his garage.

Having learnt on the small car, and become comparatively efficient, the beginner naturally aspires higher. If he is a man of moderate means, in the true sense of the term, he may be satisfied with his small car, though it be but a two-seater. The light car of good construction is cheaper to run than a horse and buggy, even after allowing for depreciation, upkeep, tires, fuel, and interest on capital, and will carry him reliably at an average speed considerably over the legal limit. The addition of a tonneau, however, to the lighter cars makes a very appreciable difference. The initial cost is higher, the wear and tear greater, tires do not last so long, and the consumption of gasolene and oil is increased.

With the three, four, and six-cylinder cars the increase is continued almost in the same proportion, and there is practically no limit upward.

As regards the choice of make only general advice can be given. Do not invest in an absolutely new type made by a firm whose members have not had experience in the motor business.

Do not trust your own judgment. Even a trained engineer cannot tell by mere inspection if a car is all right.

Do not attach too much importance to the advice of interested parties.

If you are absolutely inexperienced and have no friends to whose judgment you can trust implicity, buy on reputation. A car which has been before the public for years, and is in large demand and highly spoken of, must possess merit.

If you have gained a certain amount of knowledge by intercourse with other automobilists, or by reading, inspect the types you think most promising, get demonstrations and trial runs, and then, giving special weight to the public reputation of the firm, and the experience of those friends of yours who have owned such cars, make your decision.

Above all things avoid, if possible, the "cheap and nasty" car. It will probably cost you as much in repairs during a single season as (added to your initial expenditure) horse-power for horse-power, would have bought you the best car on the market.

As regards second-hand cars, never buy without getting expert and disinterested examination. It is worth paying a few dollars for this. Also try and find out something of the previous history of the car, and the character of the driver, as such. Many men ill-treat their cars, and the purchaser of the same second-hand is buying trouble. For this very reason second-hand cars sell cheaply, and there are grand bargains to be picked up if the would-be purchaser can only succeed in separating the chaff from the wheat.

The Question of Price.

Many people complain that the prices charged for automobiles are exorbitant. Most of them have never seen a car made, and would wonder how it could be done for the money if they had the opportunity and patience to follow all the different processes through from beginning to end. It must be remembered, too, that in comparatively few cases are models sufficiently well established, either in the factory or by fashion, to justify their being turned out in very large quantities. As time goes on, doubtless cars will become cheaper; or, rather, while the prices remain much the same, the value given for those prices will be higher.

Except in the case where cost is no object, it is best to decide in the first instance on the sum proposed to be expended, then to hunt through some such list of cars as is produced by the leading automobile journals about the period of the annual exhibitions. This will lead to a number of makes being noted as approximately right in relation to seating accommodation, price, and (now that information on motoring is becoming fairly widespread) perhaps also speed and power. The number so chosen can generally be further reduced to four or five after consulting the illustrations and descriptions of the most recent models elsewhere in this Cyclopedia, and by referring to the good or bad results obtained in reliability trials, races, long-distance records, etc. The results of speed races are not much guide as to the excellence of a model, however, except the really serious races of great length, the winning of which may be looked on as proof that the factory has a staff capable of designing, calculating and turning out a machine which can withstand the severe conditions of such a run.

Examination and Advice.

The next step is to visit the showrooms of the makers and use one's judgment, receiving with due discretion the necessarily favorable verdict which the salesman will pronounce upon his own product. At this point the real difficulty of choice comes in. If one has automobiling friends with enexperience and advice may sometimes be secured by consulting an engineer, but such a professional adviser must, of course, not be a dealer in, or interested in the sale of any cars.

It is unwise as a general rule to buy cars through the intermediary of one's own or a friend's chauffeur. It is preferable to trade direct with either the manufacturer or his agent, and, when there is a choice of agents, to buy from whatever local man is most likely to be called on to do the repairs afterwards. In either case it is often profitable to obtain and pay for skilled advice on the principle of the saying, "Advice that is not paid for is not worth having."

Every purchaser should, when ordering or buying a car, remember that he will some day want to sell it. This will often prevent the installation of some special "fad" which is the craze of the passing moment or the indulgence of some personal whim in construction which will surely detract from the selling value subsequently.

Buying a Second-hand Car.

In buying a second-hand car a very nice discrimination has to be used, for there are as many points about the second-hand automobile as there are about a stockyards horse. It is always best to obtain an expert's opinion before finally buying, unless the purchaser has already had sufficient experience to discriminate between a mechanism which has been fairly worn and one which has been torn about by bad driving and neglect. Never buy a car because of its outward appearance; a coat of paint will cover a multitude of blemishes, and it is not the finish which runs the car, though it frequently sells it to the novice. Often the result is that the owner pays for repairs in a few months a sum of money which, if added to the purchase price of the car, would have been sufficient to buy a new car. At the same time, a second-hand machine may prove an excellent educator in motor mechanics, and if the buyer happens to get hold of a really bad car, what he does not know about the details of an automobile and its tributary mechanism inside of six months is hardly worth knowing.

Examining the Frame—Having met with an apparently satisfactory vehicle, after a general inspection, the frame and wheels should first of all be subjected to a careful detailed examination. Many buyers are disposed to go for the motor and gearing alone, entirely neglecting the carriage work and frame, but as the latter has to carry the former, one should always go into that part first, so that an opinion as to the engine's capabilities of moving the vehicle can readily be formed. The stability of the entire machine centers itself upon the wheels, for no matter how good the rest may be, the whole is weak, from a traveling point of view, if the wheels are not strong enough to do the work they will be called upon to perform. Therefore, the first thing to do is to examine the wheels and their axles.

Supposing the wheels to be wood, the first tests should be for soundness generally. Grasp the rim of the wheel, and pull it towards and then push it forcibly away from you. If any give is felt or creaking heard, examine the wheel carefully to see that the spokes are tight at the hub and at the felloe or rim. If the wheel happens to have been built of imperfectly-seasoned wood, a shrinkage will probably occur, resulting in a loosening of the spokes at the felloe. More frequently the spokes are strained by inconsiderate driving over bad roads and unduly violent use of the brake many times repeated. Having tested all the wheels for soundness, next have them jacked up, and try them for wear in the bearings and for truth in running both circumferentially and laterally.

The chief test for axles is to find whether they have sunk or not; this is an easy test, for one has only to view the wheel edgewise and note if it is vertical or otherwise. If any doubt exists, a plumb line may be used. Pass a wheel which inclines outward at its top edge, but instantly reject it if it inclines inward, despite any plausible explanations from the vendor.

Springs and their Fastenings—Next examine the springs and their fastenings both to frame and axle. There is a big strain upon the shackles around the axles, and signs of springing here should be looked for. This is indicated by a cracking of the joint and an unmistakable line at the point of movement. Note that the springs lie flat upon one another, particularly at the joints. If they are apt to gape, they have been badly strained and the plates set back; the plates are therefore not doing their full share of the work, the greater part of it devolving upon the principal member.

Unsuspected Points of Wear—Points of considerable wear unsuspected and unattended to by many experienced automobilists are the bolts by which the springs are connected to the frame, particularly the free or linked end of the spring. When the car is in motion there is constant friction upon the top and bottom halves of the respective link bolts. Many owners have seen these bolts worn down by grooving one-eighth of an inch below the original diameter, and that after a few months' use. Much may be done to reduce this wear if the bolts are regularly oiled around the links and the eye at the opposite end of the spring.

The Steering Gear—The next part of the outfit to receive attention should be the steering gear. Anyone who has ever ridden in an automobile and given its operation a thought will at once realize the importance of having this as perfect as possible. The first thing to notice is the amount of backlash or free motion of the steering wheel or handle before the steering comes into operation. If the steering is of the worm and segment type, and the lost motion is found to be here, there is no radical cure for it beyond replacement. If it is on the combined screw, nut, rack and pinion type—that is, with a nut working on a screw on the steering column, the former having a rack on it engaging with a pinion—adjustment is possible by the lock-nuts at the bottom of the steering column. If the looseness is not here it will probably be found in the connection of the steering and distance rods. If these connections are made with cone screws they may be adjusted, but if plain bolts are used it means fitting new bolts, at least, to correct the error.

Brake-applying Connections—Particular attention should be directed towards the braking arrangement, especially as to its adjustment, and to the range of the hand lever applying the back wheel brakes. Unless the brake-applying connections are correctly compensated both as to the equal application of power to the brake drums and to the relative movement between the carriage body and the back axle, it will be found that while the brake may be applied with sufficient force to stop the car while the body is up on the springs, yet when it is down the lever canot be pushed down sufficiently to apply any appreciable power to the brake drums. This is because the slackness has to be taken up first by the hand lever before the band is applied to the drum. Unless sufficient travel is provided on the notched quadrant, it will be seen that with a heavy load the efficiency of the brakes is decreased under the very conditions at which it should be at its best. Sit in the car and put on the brake as hard as you can, and mark the notch in which the lever rests. Now load up the car and see how much further down the lever goes. Beyond this point there should be several notches, so as to make further application of the brake possible in contingencies. This latitude is noticeable in nearly every car fitted with cable-applied brakes, but is not so apparent in those using solid connecting rods. The pedal-applied countershaft band brake is not of so much importance, as it may easily be adjusted, and its conditions of use are not variable.

The Control Handles—Try the control handles, sparking advance, air to carbureter, and throttle if fitted; see if these are performing their various duties correctly and without too much play. At the same time, note the relative movement of each part and its lever; that is, make sure of the position of the lever when, say, the spark is retarded for starting. It is useful to know these little things when running the motor later on. It must always be remembered that a certain amount of wear has been had out of a second-hand car, and that absolutely perfect adjustment must not, and need not, be expected.

Testing the Motor—This brings us to the motor. Much has to be taken for granted here, as it is impossible to find out the exact state of an engine short of taking it down, and it is hardly likely that any owner would consent to this, unless under very exceptional circumstances. However, some very useful information may be deduced by anyone understanding the running of a motor. For those who are unable to get any experienced assistance, the following tests may be carried out, supposing that a single-cylinder motor is being tried—the multi-cylinder we will deal with later:

First test the compression. Take the starting handle and turn round the crankshaft until decided resistance is encountered; then bear heavily upon the handle, noting the strength it takes to turn the handle until the compression stroke is passed. The longer the time and the greater the strength required to overcome this resistance the better the engine is as regards the fit and wear of the cylinder and piston. It must, of course, be seen that the valve lifter is down, or the compression relief is closed, otherwise no compression will be encountered. Another thing which will sometimes be found seriously to affect compression is that, through wear on the exhaust valve seating, the valve stem has got right down on to the plunger, so that it does not close down on to its seat perfectly. This and the proper fixing of the sparking plug and other cylinder fittings are obviously things to be attended to before carrying out this test.

Connecting Rod Bearings—The next test is for wear in the connecting rod bearings; this, in some cases, is very difficult to carry out. Where it is practicable to fix the starting handle, or a long wrench to the crankshaft end, a gentle movement backward and forward will disclose any looseness in these bearings. Failing this test, the engine should be listened to very carefully while starting up, running slow, and stopping. If a distinct and recurring knocking noise is heard, it may very safely be assumed that the connecting-rod bearings are loose, and require taking up or renewing. If the gearing is inclosed and cannot be viewed, remove the contact breaker cover, and by moving the cam backward and forward a rough estimate of wear can be formed. If these wheels have been badly cut in the first place, the wear may amount to such proportions as would materially affect both the lifting of the exhaust valve and the amount of firing. Of course, the latter may be corrected by advancing the contact, but the late opening of the exhaust valve cannot be remedied without re-setting the wheel on the shaft.

The Water Circulating System—If the motor is water-cooled, examine the water jacket for cracks, particularly around the head and valve chamber, where the jacket is cast in one with a solid-headed cylinder. When the cylinder and head are cast separately with their water jackets there is less risk of such cracks appearing. Attention should next be directed towards the water circulating pump, where such is fitted, and if driven by belt or friction wheel, the spindle should be felt to see that it is not too loose. It is as well to remove the stuffing box nut around the spindle, for at this point there is usually a lot of wear taking place, and it is just as well to know exactly in what condition the pump spindle is. It will probably save a lot of trouble later on. Look over the water pipes and connections. A badly-dented tube resists the passage of water, and, of course, affects the cooling of the cylinder to a considerable extent, that is, if it be a main delivery or return tube. The flexible connections of the water pipes should be of rubber hose, and should be free from leaks. It would be absurd to look at trivial points such as this with too critical an eye, yet beginners often make a trouble of a point like this, while they would say nothing about a lubricator which would not work, simply because they did not know it was out of order. This is where the experienced man comes in.

Testing Ignition—The electric ignition apparatus should receive particular attention, as it is sometimes a little misunderstanding of this part which brings a really good car into the market. The most important part of the apparatus is the contact breaker or commutator. As there is a general misunderstanding of these terms, it will be as well to state their differences here. The contact breaker is a piece of mechanism in which two parts are put into contact with one another for a time, and are then parted. A commutator is a disk of insulating material having on its periphery metallic pieces in a like number to that of the cylinder. Bearing upon the disk is a brush of copper gauze, sheet copper, or steel, which, when the metallic pieces in the commutator pass beneath it, cause the current to pass. As the commutator is now perhaps more frequently employed than the contact breaker, we will use this term, but it must be understood that any remarks apply to both equally. The first thing is to see that the commutator is set correctly. To do this, relieve the cylinder compression, and turn the starting handle until the plunger rises to lift the exhaust valve; continue turning until the plunger drops. Now turn the handle round one revolution exactly, at which point the commutator should be about to come into action, that is, when it is set right back. Then move the sparking advance lever up, and note the amount of travel the brush has around the commutator; this represents the limits of ignition. A more definite method of finding the point of ignition is, when possible, to drop a stiff wire through the compression tap, letting it rest upon the top of the piston.

Batteries and Wiring—The wiring and all the connections should be examined most carefully, especially as to the cleanliness of the terminals and the soundness of the insulation around the wires. The chief points for inspecting the latter are at places where it bends round any part of the mechanism. At such places the vibration to which the wire is subjected frequently causes the insulation to be worn away, resulting in annoying short circuits, and it is such defects as these which, as we said before, cause good machines to appear in the market. Where possible, look at the accumulator or battery plates to see they are not bent, as they may possibly be if they have been discharged too rapidly or too low. Also note at the same time if the plates themselves are complete; it sometimes happens that some of the paste falls from the plates, and if this happens to lodge between a positive and negative plate it sets up an internal "short," causing no little trouble.

Carbureter Efficiency—The carbureter should be examined to see that the air adjustment, float, and throttle valve (if fitted) work freely. Start the engine and while it is running slowly listen for any knocking or grinding sounds. Next, get a good mixture, and with the throttle full open gradually advance the ignition, noting if the engine answers to it well. Retard the spark, or cut off the current, and again listen for any knocks. When the engine stops, start it up again, and advance the spark about half or two-thirds of its travel, and then try varying the speed by means of the throttle valve. It will be as well at this stage to see that the cooling water has not become unduly heated, for if it keeps fairly cool while the engine is running with the car stationary, it will be certain to be more effective while the vehicle is moving. No indication of the power of the engine can be ascertained while the engine is running light.

Examining Multi-cylinder Engines—Up to the present we have been dealing solely with a single-cylinder motor, so we will now pass on to the extended tests required for a multi-cylinder one. Each cylinder should be tested for compression in the same way as previously described for a single-cylinder. The compression in each cylinder should be, as nearly as possible, equal. As the two-to-one gear wheels are usually of ample proportions, deterioration here may be regarded as a negative quantity. The ends of both crankshaft and camshaft being within easy access, these may be tried for wear, while the opposite end of the crankshaft may be similarly tried by means of the flywheel. The examination of the commutator, as regards its position, is not of such great importance in this case on account of the reduced wear on the two-to-one gear wheels. The remainder of the mechanism should be inspected and tested in the same manner as for a single-cylinder engine.

The Lubrication—The lubrication of the engine is of the greatest importance, and this should therefore he looked to with a very critical eye. The methods of supplying lubricant are varied. In some engines the oil is passed through to the crank chamber in quantities by means of a force pump; in others it is supplied regularly drop by drop by a drip lubricator. These are the more useful methods. With the force pump lubricator it is sufficient to see that the pump is acting correctly, and that its piping is complete and not leaking at any joints. In the drip feed lubricator a more careful examination is needed, as there are adjustment details to be looked to, for it is most important that the feed be regulated to suit the fluid conditions of the oil. If the drip valves are found to act correctly, then look over the pipes for dents or fractures. The pipes should in this case be of fairly large diameter, so as not to interfere with the free flowing of the oil. There are a variety of mechanical oil feeds fitted, and these should be noted for correct functioning while the engine is running.

Transmission Considerations—We next arrive at the transmission gear, but this we must deal with very broadly, as there are so many adaptations of the various systems. The first part of the transmission is the clutch. With the hand, depress the clutch pedal and see that the driven portion is withdrawn clear of the driver without any excessive force being used. In the case of leather to metal clutches, if the male cone can be withdrawn sufficiently to examine the leather facing, it should be seen if this is in good order and not worn down too thin. While the male cone is out of engagement the clutchshaft should be tried for wear by lifting it at the cone. It should also be noted that there is provision made for adjusting both the clutch and the clutch pedal.

The Change Speed Gear—It will be necessary to lift the lid off the gear-box to inspect the change speed gear wheels. The teeth of these wheels should show a brightly burnished surface on the faces, but not on the tops and bottoms. By faces is meant the breadth of the teeth which engage with the opposite wheel. If they show as brightly at the tooth bottom as they do on the faces, they have been intermeshed too deeply in the first place, and there is likely to be excessive wear. If they show dark or lightly touched surfaces, they have been correctly set, and they should be in good running order; in fact, they will probably be better than new. Each of the wheels should be looked at all the way round to ascertain that no teeth are broken. If the sliding type of gear—that is, a type where the wheels are slid into engagement sidewise—be in the car under notice, the edges of the teeth should be looked to. If the car has been in good hands, the teeth will show brightly on their engaging sides; but if the driver has been at all clumsy it will probably be found that the teeth are badly chipped at these points.

The speed changing movements should all be closely watched while manipulating the actuating lever. The wheels on the sliding sleeve should move deliberately and accurately into their corresponding wheel—that is, provided the teeth are not opposite one another. The edges of the wheels should be in a perfect line, not one overhanging the other; if this is the case, it indicates a lot of lost motion in the connections between the sleeves and the actuating lever. A certain amount of latitude is permissible here, but the movement should not be more than what might be termed "a little free." If there is a lot of backlash there is something wrong somewhere, and it should be carefully looked for with a view of correction. If the total width of one wheel exceeds that of the other, as is sometimes the case, particularly with the reversing gear, then it does not follow that something must necessarily be wrong.

Points of Strain and Wear—The bolting up of the gear-box

to the frame also should be inspected, particularly for signs of straining. Its oil-retaining and dust-excluding capacities should be attended to, otherwise trouble is likely to follow. After the shaking up of a few thousand miles the lid of the box sometimes develops a tendency to rattle by reason of the catches working loose; where studs or bolts and nuts are used for this purpose, there is no fear of the lid coming adrift.

The countershaft bearings and differential gear should be looked to and tried as far as possible, and side chains, if any, carefully inspected. These and the sprocket wheels should be examined most carefully, as they are the last stage but one in the chain-drive transmission system, and, moreover, often have to run entirely exposed. Hard, gritty, sandy mud acts as an abrasive upon both chain and sprockets, cutting them about very badly, if the car has had much running in bad weather in sandy districts. The forward or wearing side of the teeth is likely in time to become concave in form instead of convex, thus interfering with the chain leaving the wheel freely. As to the chains, the principal parts are the side links upon which the greater strain comes. If these appear to be cut or distorted and want renewing, it should have an effect on the price of the car.

The propeller-shaft joints, bevels, differential gear and driving ends of the rear axle should all be tested for play. How to do this properly should be learned by every conscientious driver.

Wear and Tear Considerations—It should always be borne in mind that one must discriminate between fair wear and tear and bad usage. The results of fair wear and tear will always be found in a second-hand car and cannot very well be objected to, but results of bad usage should be noted as likely to cause future trouble. In such parts as the steering gear, governor, carbureter, ignition system and other connections there will usually be some looseness due to use, and allowance must be made for this. It is only excessive wear, the result of misuse, or bad fitting, that needs careful examination before deciding upon the purchase of a second-hand car which exhibits such symptoms.

When one has examined a likely car it is well to make a fairly liberal estimate for adjustments and replacements which may be thought necessary, and in calculating cost this amount should be added to the purchase price of the car. As already stated, the sum required for alterations, repairs and replacements in a second-hand car, added to the purchase price, would frequently suffice to buy a new car.

Choice of Tires—The buyer of a new car is often offered the option of several kinds or makes of pneumatic tires. As the tire question is a very important one in relation to automobiling it is advisable that every owner and intending purchaser should fully inform himself as to the various styles and brands of tire in the market so as to exercise a wise discretion in making his choice. Experience is of course the best guide in this and other matters connected with motoring, and he who lacks personal experience must needs rely on that of his friends or on the word and reputation of the manufacturer and dealer. But it should always be borne in mind that a poor tire is dear at any price.

Reliable figures can be obtained as to the proper size of tire to use on a car of a certain weight and horse-power. The objects sought for in selecting a size of tire for a car are stated as follows:

1. To obtain the comfort, the absence of personal fatigue, and the protection from wear and tear to machinery which a pneumatic tire can give, while at the same time attending to the considerations named in the next two paragraphs.

2. To avoid constantly bursting the tire cover by the wear induced by excessive bending of the rubber and canvas side walls. This occurs if the tire is too slight in section for the load, the horse-power or the speed employed.

3. To secure just such a size of tire that the tire bill is the minimum compatible with comfortable use, that is, not too large in section, nor of too big a diameter, as this makes steering difficult and is unnecessarily expensive in first cost, and

yet (which is far the more common fault) not of too small a diameter, as the running costs due to bursts then become prohibitive.

PART XV.

CHANGE SPEED GEAR—VARIOUS FORMS.

The internal combustion engine exerts its maximum power at a constant speed; consequently, variation of pace is possible only between narrow limits from the motor itself, and recourse has to be had to the mechanism known as the change speed gear, in order to obtain the necessary range of flexibility required.

This consists fundamentally of a reducing gear, by which the high rate of revolution of the motor crank shaft is modified to a lower speed on a secondary shaft, from which the road wheels are driven. The ratio between the rate of revolution of the motor shaft and the speed of the secondary shaft is capable of alteration, generally in a series of steps and between fixed limits.

Ordinary change speed gear, such as is in every-day use at present, consists generally of a series of gear wheels varying in size, pairs of which can be engaged one with another whilst the remainder are idle. The mechanical methods by which this can be done are limited in number, and the following list indicates the broad headings under which change-speed gear principles act:

1. By sliding the wheels into or out of mesh, either separately or on a sleeve.

2. By having the gears constantly in mesh, and determining the working pair by means of a sliding feather, which locks any required wheels to the shaft.

3. Constantly meshing gears rendered live by means of

clutches, either frictional or expanding, or by positive or dog clutch engagements.

4. Epicycloidal gears, where the changes are obtained by gripping and releasing the various members.

These four classes comprise the standard systems, but almost every maker of note has some specialty of his own, which, though varying but slightly from a standard pattern, would necessitate a lengthy description for its complete comprehension.

The first of these four classes of change speed gear is found in the Panhard and other chain-driven cars, is typical and comprises simply a pair of shafts inclosed in an air-tight box, one driven through the medium of the friction clutch from the engine, and the other driven from the first by means of gear wheels.

The most satisfactory arrangement of variable speed mechanism comprises a motor powerful enough to take all small gradients on the top gear, combined with a transmission providing at least two lower gears for hills properly so-called.

TRANSMISSION AND VARIABLE GEARING.

Selective Sliding Gears.

The method of sliding gear wheels into mesh with each other endways seems, from an engineering point of view, a barbarous system. It is remarkable, however, that in practice it has been proved most successful for change speed gears in motor cars. The different ways in which this method of gear changing can be arranged is remarkable, and we shall deal with several systems in order.

The Panhard Type—The Panhard was the earliest example of the type of change speed gear in which the gear wheels were arranged to slide endways. It is still used on a number of cars, and has given remarkable results, but modifications of it have lately been introduced which are becoming rather more popular, though the principle embodied in the Panhard gear is that which is found in practically every type of sliding gear on the market.

In the accompanying figures, which are purely diagrammatic, we have a four-speed Panhard type of gear.

The different figures from one to four show the gear in operation in four different speeds; as the reference letters are alike in the four diagrams, there will be no difficulty in following the procedure.

Shaft X is the shaft which is driven by the engine. It will be noticed that it is carried in two bearings—one at each end in the gear box, and that between those two bearings the shaft is square shape.

It is on the squared part of the shaft that the four wheels A, B, C, and D are mounted. They are so mounted that

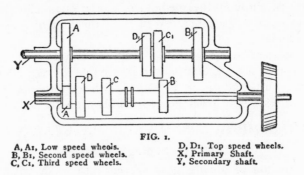

FIG. 1.

A, A₁, Low speed wheels.   D, D₁, Top speed wheels.
B, B₁, Second speed wheels.   X, Primary Shaft.
C, C₁, Third speed wheels.   Y, Secondary shaft.

they can slide on the square, being pushed along in either direction by a fork which encircles the collar shown between B and C. The fork which operates this collar is connected by means of rods to the change speed gear lever operated by the driver.

It must be remembered that A, B, C, and D are always relatively in the same position to each other, because they are mounted on one single sleeve which slides along the squared part of the shaft X, so that any movement of the collar in either direction will move the whole four gear wheels.

Outside of the gear box is seen, in diagrammatic form, the male portion of the clutch which puts shaft X into driving communication with the engine shaft. X is termed the primary gear shaft. Lying parallel with it, and also in two bearings in the gear box, is shaft Y, which is termed the secondary shaft. It is from shaft Y that power is transmitted to the differential box. On Y are wheels A1, C1, B1, and D1. These wheels are of such diameters as to mesh respectively with A, B, C, and D on the shaft X. They are rigidly attached to the shaft Y, and can neither move around nor along it. In this respect they are different from the wheels A, B, C, and D on shaft X. These wheels cannot move around the shaft, but can move along it. In the position shown in Fig. 1 the gear wheel A is in mesh with gear wheel A1.

If, now, the engine drives the shaft X, the wheel A will

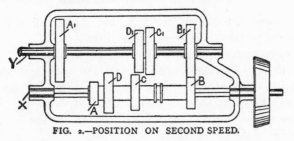

FIG. 2.—POSITION ON SECOND SPEED.

rotate shaft Y through the medium of A1, and Y will rotate the differential box and drive the car; but since A is considerably less in diameter than A1, it is obvious that the car will travel comparatively slowly relatively to the speed of the engine shaft, which is the speed of X. This is the low gear.

Supposing, now, it is desired to make the difference between the speed of the engine and the speed of the shaft Y relatively less; if we bring the sleeve carrying wheels A, D, C, and B to the right in our diagram, the wheel A will come out of mesh with A1, and B will come into mesh with B1. B1 is smaller in diameter than A1, while B is larger in diameter than A; therefore, although B is smaller than B1, shaft Y will still rotate at less speed than shaft X. This will give us the second speed. This is shown in Fig. 2.

To get on the third speed we must slide the sleeve on shaft X still further to the right until B comes out of engagement with B1, and C comes into engagement with C1. This is shown in Fig. 3. It will be seen here also that C1 is larger in diameter than C, so that shaft Y will still be mov-

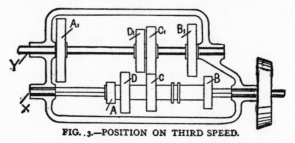

FIG. .3.—POSITION ON THIRD SPEED.

ing at a less speed than shaft X, but there will not be so great a difference as in the case of Fig. 2.

To get on to top gear, the sleeve on shaft X must be moved still further to the right until D and D1 come into engagement with each other. Now, D and D1 are of the same diameter, therefore shaft X and shaft Y will be rotating at the same speed, and the engine will be driving the bevel pinion on the differential at its own speed.

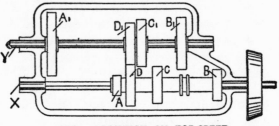

FIG. 4.—POSITION ON TOP SPEED.

In this method of arranging the sliding gears there can never be a position in which the engine drives direct on to the shaft which drives the differential. That is to say, there is no direct drive on the Panhard type of gear.

As regards the reverse—which is not shown in our diagram—there is a wheel mounted on a third shaft which engages with A1 and A respectively—thus reversing the direction of motion—shafts X and Y now revolving in the same instead of the opposite direction to each other. This gives the reverse gear.

In the Panhard system (as used up till very lately on all models of Panhard cars, and which has given its name to a type of gear) it is usual to have a countershaft with sprocket wheels and chain drive, and in such cases the secondary shaft Y carries on its end, and inside the gear box, the bevel pinion which engages with the crown wheel on the differential shaft. The same system is adopted on other cars in which the shaft Y terminates in a universal joint, connecting it up to either a cardan or a propeller shaft, and transmitting the power to a live axle which contains the differential.

The Mercedes Type—The Mercedes type of gear takes its name from a gear which was introduced on one of the earlier Mercedes cars. The word "Mercedes" has now become a generic term for gears which incorporate the system introduced by the Mercedes Company. It uses the sliding type of gear—the gears coming into engagement with each other endways—but it has this great advantage, that, by using two pairs of sliding wheels instead of all four sliding together, as in the Panhard type, the shaft on which the gear wheels are mounted can be kept short. It has also another distinct advantage in the fact that a direct drive from engine to back axle can be got without the power having to be transmitted through the second shaft. In such cases, of course, instead of having two sets of gears in operation, only one set is used between the engine and the back axle on the top speed —that set is the bevel and crown wheel of the differential.

The gear box of the 35 h.p. Talbot car, shown in Fig. 5, may be taken as an example of the latest type of the Mercedes principle.

It will here be seen that we have a primary and a secondary shaft, just as we have in the case of the Panhard. The primary shaft is shown at PGS, the secondary shaft at SGS. Sometimes SGS is known as the lay shaft. The primary gear shaft is not directly connected to the engine or the clutch, but at the left-hand end in our illustration it will be seen that it is surrounded by the sleeve IGS, which we may term the initial gear sleeve. This sleeve is driven by the engine, and, with the gears in the position shown in our illustration, it is not in connection at all with the primary gear shaft PGS, but will simply revolve about it on the ball

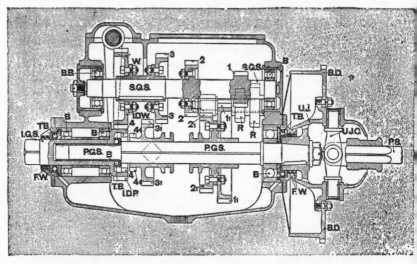

FIG. 5. –VERTICAL SECTION OF TALBOT GEAR BOX.

I G S, Initial gear sleeve.
I D P, Intermediate driving pinion.
I D W, Intermediate driven wheel.
S G S, Secondary gear shaft.
1 and 1₁, Driving and driven wheels of first speed
2 and 2₁, Driving and driven wheels of second speed
3 and 3₁, Driving and driven wheels of third speed.
4 and 4₁, Driving and driven parts of fourth speed direct driving clutch.

P G S, Primary gear shaft.
R R, Reverse pinions.
B B, Ball bearings.
T B, Thrust ball bearings.
F W, Felt oil-retaining washers.
U J, Fore part of universal joint.
B D, Brake drum.
U J C, Universal joint coupling.
P S, Propeller shaft.

bearings B B. The power from the engine is transmitted to this sleeve. On its right-hand end it is provided with external and internal teeth, the external teeth being explained by the letters IDP (which stand for intermediate driving pinion). Now, this pinion is in constant engagement with the gear wheel IDW (which stands for intermediate driven wheel) on the secondary gear shaft SGS; that is to say, so long as the engine rotates the sleeve IGS, it will also rotate the gear wheel IDW, and, therefore, the secondary gear shaft SGS and all the wheels upon it—all these four wheels being permanently fixed in position and incapable of rotating except with the shaft.

Imagine, now, the gear in the position we show it and the engine running. IGS is rotating and driving with it at a much lesser speed the shaft SGS, because the pinion IDP is less in diameter than the gear wheel IDW.

It will be seen that no gear wheels on the shaft SGS are in gear with the shaft PGS, so that the shaft PGS will not be rotated by the engine, and as this shaft is connected by the universal joint UJC to the propeller shaft of the rear axle PS, the engine will not be driving the car.

On the primary gear shaft PGS are two sets of gear wheels. On the right are gear wheels 1_1 and 2_1, which can be slid independently along the gear shaft because they are on a square which, while preventing them rotating, allows them to slide laterally along it. Then we have the gear wheels 3_1 and 4_1 on a similar sleeve, capable of sliding along the shaft, but not rotating upon it.

In order to allow the engine to drive the shaft PGS, and in view of the fact that the shaft SGS is constantly rotating while the engine is running, it is necessary to slide some one or other of the wheels on shaft PGS into engagement with one or other of the wheels on shaft SGS.

It will be obvious that the smallest wheel on shaft SGS, if put into engagement with the largest wheel on shaft PGS, will give us the greatest difference between the speed of the two shafts, and, therefore, the greatest difference between the speed of the engine and the speed of the propeller shaft which drives the car.

Hence, by moving the sleeve which carries 1_1 and 2_1 so that the wheel 1_1 comes into engagement with wheel 1, we get the first, or lowest, speed—the power being transmitted through IDP, IDW, 1 and 1_1 to the shaft PGS and the propeller shaft PS.

If the sleeve is moved to the left, so that 2_1 comes into engagement with 2, we still have a smaller wheel on shaft SGS in gear with a larger wheel on shaft PGS; but the difference is less, and, therefore, the difference between the speed of the engine and the speed of the car will be reduced. This is the second speed, the power being transmitted through IDP, IDW, 2 and 2_1 to shaft PGS.

For forward speeds these are the only two functions which are performed by the sleeve carrying the two wheels 2_1 and 1_1.

If it is desired to get from the second to the third speed, the sleeve carrying 2_1 and 1_1 must be returned to a position in which neither of the wheels engage with their corresponding wheels on the secondary gear shaft. The gate mechanism, which we shall shortly explain, allows us to do this, and to leave that pair of wheels locked in the neutral position. The next movement of the hand-lever brings the wheel 3_1 on its sleeve to the right, so that it gears with 3 on the secondary gear shaft. The engine will then drive through IDP, IDW, 3 and 3_1, thus rotating the primary gear shaft PGS—still driving the car at a reduced speed compared with that of the engine. This is the third speed.

For the fourth speed, in which the engine will drive the propeller shaft at the same speed at which it is turning itself, we must move the sleeve carrying wheel 3_1 and 4_1 to the left. 4_1 is not really a gear wheel, although it is exactly the same shape as a gear wheel, but it meshes completely into all the teeth of the internal wheel 4, forming a clutch between the primary gear shaft and the initial gear sleeve. The engine, as before, will rotate the intermediate gear sleeve IGS, and as 4_1 is completely housed in 4, the primary gear shaft PGS and the initial gear sleeve IGS driven by the engine become as one, and rotate at the same speed; meanwhile, the secondary gear shaft rotates idly, having no effect on the transmission of the power.

As regards the reverse, there are two wheels R and R shown in faint outline. These wheels are mounted on a separate shaft underneath the primary and the secondary gear shafts. By moving these two wheels R and R to the left, wheel R will come into engagement with wheel 1 on the secondary gear shaft, while the lesser wheel R will come into engagement with wheel 1 on the primary gear shaft, thus reversing the motion, and making the primary gear shaft rotate in the opposite direction to the initial gear sleeve driven by the engine. This gives the reverse gear.

It will be seen that in this gear the secondary gear shaft, with all its wheels, is constantly rotating even when the gear is so arranged that there is a direct drive on top gear. Several gears on the Mercedes principle have been devised to overcome this difficulty and to put the secondary gear shaft entirely out of operation while the high speed gear is in operation.

Gate Control Mechanism.

In those types of gear which, on the Mercedes principle, as we have described, use two pairs of sliding wheels instead of only one set of sliding wheels, as in the Panhard, a gate control mechanism is usually adopted. It will be seen that it is necessary that two of the speeds utilize one pair of sliding wheels to slide into engagement with one or other of two wheels, and that the other two speeds use the other pair of sliding wheels. This could be achieved by adopting two operating hand levers, one for each pair of sliding gears; but this would be a disadvantage in that it might confuse the driver at a critical moment, and he might, unless some intricate form of interlocking arrangement were fitted, accidentally put two gears into mesh at the same time. In any case, it would compel him to move one lever to disengage one set of gears, and then move another lever to engage another set.

In order to overcome this difficulty, a gate change and selector bar arrangement is usually applied. These appliances may be designed in different ways, but the principle underlying them all is that which is illustrated, in a purely diagrammatic form, in Fig. 6. A is the change speed lever on the end of the shaft F, which is free to oscillate in a sleeve G, or any bearing equivalent to the sleeve G, which is attached to some part of the car. It is also free to move endways inside the sleeve G. The extent of its oscillation in G is determined by the length of the slots in quadrant B, through which the lever passes. It will be seen that the quadrant B has two slots C and D, with a gate between them E. Now, the lever can only pass through from one slot to the other when it is in a position opposite to E, so that the combined

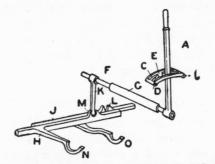

FIG. 6.—DIAGRAMMATIC VIEW OF A SELECTOR BAR AND GATE CONTROL MECHANISM.

A, Change speed lever.
B, Quadrant through which lever A moves.
C and D, Slots in the quadrant through which the lever moves.
E, Gate or opening between the two slots in quadrant B.
F, Oscillating shaft to which levers A and K are rigidly attached.
G, Sleeve through which shaft F may be moved endways and in which it may be oscillated.

H, One of the selector bars.
J, The other selector bar.
K, Selector lever operating bars H and J.
L, Slot in selector bar J.
M, Slot in selector bar H.
N and O, Forks on the selector bars H and J which engage with the sliding wheels in the gear box.

width of the two slots determines the distance of travel of which the shaft F is capable inside the sleeve G.

At the other end of shaft F is seen a lever K, which is rigidly attached to it, and this lever K not only oscillates with the oscillation of the shaft F, but is also moved endways with F. H and J are two bars which are free to slide endways in guides, which, for the sake of clearness, are not shown in our diagram. These bars have projecting from them slotted lugs L and M. These slotted lugs are of such a shape that the end of the lever K can be moved into them endways, and will engage with them in such a way that they can be moved lengthways by any movement of the lever K. These bars are known as "selector bars," and the lever K as the "selector lever." It is the function of lever K to select and operate the gear wheels which it is required to move.

The bar H has, formed with it, an arm having at its end a fork N. This fork engages with a collar on one pair of sliding wheels in the gear box. Similarly, the bar J has an arm terminating in a fork O, which engages with the collar on the other pair of sliding gears in the gear box. In the position shown the gear change lever A is in the forward slot in the quadrant, so that the lever K is in engagement with the slot in the bar H. By moving the lever backward and forward in the slot D in the quadrant, the bar H will be moved backward and forward, and will, of course, carry with it, through the medium of the fork N, one pair of gear wheels. When lever A is in the forward position in the slot D, one of these gear wheels will be in engagement with a gear wheel on the secondary shaft. Similarly, when it is moved to the left-hand end of the slot, it will cause the other wheel of the pair to engage with another wheel on the secondary shaft. It will be seen that this will give two different gears.

When lever A is moved into such a position that it comes opposite the gate E between the two slots C and D, this particular pair of wheels which the bar H controls will be in a position in which they are out of engagement with their fellow-wheels on the secondary shaft. When in that position, the slot M in bar H will come opposite the slot L in bar J. If, now, the lever is pushed through the gate E into the slot C, the lever K will similarly be pushed through out of slot M in bar H into slot L in bar J. Bar H will then be left in the same position in which bar J is in our illustration, and the operation of the hand lever A will only control the bar J; that is to say, the lever has been made to select another bar in place of bar H. If, now, the lever is operated as before (but, of course, in this case in slot C of the quadrant), bar L will be moved backward and forward, and, through the medium of the fork O attached to it, it will move the second pair of sliding wheels. When in the forward position, it will engage one wheel with its fellow on the secondary shaft. When it is in the backward position, it will engage the other wheel of the pair with its fellow on the secondary shaft. In order that while one bar is being operated and the other lies idle the second one cannot be moved so as to engage the other pair of wheels, spring tops are usually provided which hold the bar not in operation so that it cannot move endways, so as to prevent two gears being put into operation at the same time, which, of course, would be disastrous.

To make our diagram as simple as possible, we have left out the arrangement for the reverse, but this consists of a third slot in the quadrant parallel with the slots C and D, and also having a gate similar to E through which the hand lever can be pushed. It can easily be imagined that lever K will then be carried past the slot in the bar L into a slot in a third bar which operates the gear wheel which gives the reverse motion.

It will be understood that the action of this device is such that the lever cannot be moved from one slot to the other without leaving the bar, with which it formerly engaged, in the neutral position, and the wheels consequently out of gear.

This selector bar arrangement is carried out in different ways on different cars. Sometimes the whole arrangement is incorporated in the gear box; in other cases the selector bars and the selector lever are arranged in a separate case, and the rods are extended from this case to the gear box.

Friction Gearing.

Many attempts have been made to get a variable gear for motor cars which would give an infinite variation between maximum and minimum, and this has generally been done by adopting some sort of friction drive. The friction of the periphery of one wheel on the face of another, and sliding the one wheel across the other, has been utilized on many occasions. In its simplest form this gear is shown in Figs. 7 and 8. Fig. 7 represents it in plan and Fig. 8 in elevation.

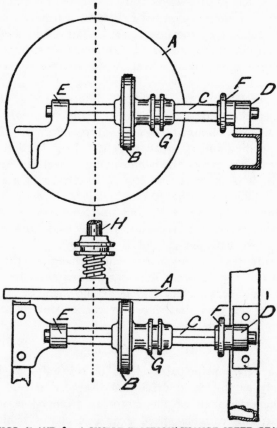

FIGS. **7** AND **8.**—A SIMPLE FRICTION CHANGE SPEED GEAR.

A, Flat faced wheel driven by engine.
B, Friction wheel sliding across face A.
C, Shaft which carries friction wheel B.

D and E, Bearings carrying shaft C.
F, Chain sprocket to transmit power.
G, Collar for moving wheel B.
H, Collar and spring pressing wheel A up against wheel B.

In both figures A represents a large wheel with a flat face, driven by the engine. B represents a wheel having on its periphery a leather friction surface, which comes in contact

with the wheel A—best shown in the plain view, Fig. 7. B
is mounted on a shaft C, and this shaft is carried in bearings
D and E, and at one end a chain wheel F is keyed to it, by
means of which the power is transmitted to the differential.
B is capable of sliding along the shaft C, which at that part
is square, but not of rotating upon it. It is slid along the
shaft by means of the collar G. H is a coil spring which
presses the engine-driven wheel A up against the friction
wheel B.

By moving B along the face of A, different ratios of gearing between the shaft which carries A and the shaft which
carries B may be obtained, and, therefore, different ratios between the engine and the road wheels. If the friction wheel
B is moved right across the center of the wheel A to the opposite side, it is obvious that it will be driven in a reverse
direction, which gives the reverse gear. A lever is used to
operate the sliding wheel B, and another lever is used to
take off the pressure of the spring H so as to release frictional pressure between A and B, thus acting as a clutch.
The pressure may be taken off when changing the gear,
though in this type of gear it is not always necessary. Our
diagrams show only a very simple arrangement of this kind
of change speed gear, but, however carried out in practice,
the principle remains the same.

Chain Drive Gearing.

There are two principal systems of transmission, known
respectively as the chain drive and the gear drive. In the
former the crankshaft of the motor is arranged lengthwise
of the car, the variable speed gear box comes behind the
clutch, and motion is communicated to a transverse, balance-
geared shaft, the ends of which are connected by chain gearing with the respective driving road wheels. The greater
part of the clutchshaft is of square section, and on this part
is mounted a sleeve furnished with four spur wheels of different diameters. Another shaft, called the gearshaft, is set
parallel to the clutchshaft and has fixed to it four spur wheels,

proportioned to those on the sleeve. The sleeve can be moved lengthwise, by a hand lever, so as to bring any one wheel thereon into engagement with the fellow wheel on the gearshaft. The different wheels in each set are so spaced apart that it is impossible to engage two pairs of wheels at the same time. So in changing from one gear to another the parts pass through an "out of gear" position; and this is how they must be set for starting the motor, and also for allowing the motor to run while the car is making a temporary stop. Otherwise it would be necessary to hold the clutch out of engagement all the while the car was stopped and the engine running.

The average size of the wheels on the sleeve is less than the average size of the wheels on the gearshaft, so that, as a rule, part of the gear reduction between the motor and the road wheels is made here. When the largest wheel on the sleeve is meshed with the smallest wheel on the gearshaft the car will be driven at its highest (in this case the fourth) speed. And as each smaller gear wheel on the sleeve is meshed with its fellow on the gearshaft, the gear will be reduced, through the third and second speeds to the first speed, in turn. The "first" speed means the lowest in automobiling. On the rear end of the gearshaft is a bevel wheel which gears with a corresponding bevel wheel on the balance-geared countershaft.

The Reverse Motion.

The reverse motion in a chain drive gear is often obtained by bringing a third wheel or pinion into gear with a wheel on the sleeve and a wheel on the gearshaft, these two wheels being of such sizes that they cannot mesh directly with each other. The introduction of the pinion, of course, causes the sleeve and the gearshaft to turn in the same direction; while, when the other wheels thereon engage directly with each other, they turn in opposite directions. The later form of reversing gear only provides one backward speed, and this should be a slow one; indeed, it is best to make it a lower gear than any of the forward ones, as then if a hill is encountered that even the first forward speed is too high for, the car can sometimes be driven up backward. The old form of reversing gear gave as many speeds backward as forward, and most, if not all, of them were too high for ordinary use. The driver who accidentally reversed on his fourth speed had quite an exciting time of it.

The Side Chains.

The outer ends of the balance-geared cross-shaft or counter-shaft are generally separate from and coupled up to the main portions by flexible joints. A chain wheel or sprocket is fixed to each of these end pieces, and corresponding chain wheels are mounted on the driving road wheels, which turn freely on a fixed axle. Endless pitch chains run round the pairs of chain wheels. Adjustable "radius rods" are provided for keeping the wheels of each chain at a fixed distance apart, notwithstanding the movement of the carriage springs; and these rods also provide means for adjusting the tension of the chains. The chains being so close to the road wheels were very much exposed to wet, dirt and grit, and consequently often wore out quickly, but in modern cars they are satisfactorily incased. A further reduction of the speed ratio is made in the chain gearing, the sprockets on the counter-shaft being smaller than those on the road wheels.

The original chain drive gear being very bulky, attempts have been made to modify it so as to reduce the size. One of the most successful consists in dividing the sleeve into two parts. This allows the spacing apart of the wheels to be reduced, and also enables the gear to be changed from one speed to another without passing through the intermediate gears.

Another device consists in packing the wheels in each set close together and arranging the respective pairs in permanent engagement. All the wheels on one of the shafts are normally loose, and each is fixed as required by a rod carrying a key or feather sliding in the shaft. This is very compact, and it gets over the sliding of the wheels into mesh with one another, but the strains on the key and keyways are very severe, though removed from the teeth.

The chain drive type of gearing is seldom found except on the larger cars and those of the buggy type.

The Gear Drive.

The cardan, arbor, propeller-shaft or live-axle gear is common on light cars and has made very rapid headway on the heavy ones. The arrangement of the motor and clutch is similar to that described above, but the variable speed gear is devised with the clutchshaft and gearshaft in line; and for the top speed these two shafts are coupled together and rotate as one, the power being transmitted direct instead of through spur wheels. There are at least three speeds forward and one reverse, the two lower speeds and the reverse being obtained by the spur wheels. The construction is very ingenious, and may be described thus: The rear end of the clutchshaft and the forward end of the gearshaft telescope into each other. The gearshaft is made of square section, and on it is mounted a sleeve carrying two spur wheels of different sizes. On the forward end of the sleeve are two strong dogs or projections, while on the rear end of the clutchshaft is fixed a wide spur pinion having two recesses in its back face. A second gearshaft is mounted parallel to the first, and on this are fixed three forward spur wheels corresponding in diameter to the two on the first gearshaft and the one on the clutchshaft.

For the top speed the clutchshaft and first gearshaft are coupled together by moving the sleeve forward until the dogs thereon enter the recesses in the spur wheel on the clutchshaft. This is the "direct drive," and is so called because no power is lost by transmitting it through the second gearshaft; indeed, in some forms of the gear, the second shaft is not even rotated when the top speed is in. For the two lower speeds, the sleeve is moved back so as to disengage the dog clutch and bring one of the wheels on the sleeve into gear with the fellow wheel on the second shaft. Now the power is transmitted from the pinion on the clutchshaft to the largest wheel of the second shaft, and then back from one of the smaller wheels on this shaft to the wheel in gear with it on the sleeve, and so to the first gearshaft. This is not unlike the backgear of a lathe. For reversing purposes a fourth wheel on the second shaft is geared with the larger wheel on the sleeve through an intermediate wheel.

This form of variable gear is now often employed in conjunction with a balance geared cross-shaft and side-chains. On powerful cars it is not infrequently modified to give four speeds, and then the third speed is sometimes made to give the direct drive, if the fourth is too high for general use.

In nearly all cars the gear is changed by a hand lever pivoted at the right-hand side of the frame and working in a slotted quadrant. Recesses in the quadrant receive a safety catch worked by a finger lever on the hand lever, and hold the latter in the different positions to which it is set in changing gear. The gate-change quadrant is so called from its having two or more slots side by side, and an opening or gate between them through which the lever is moved with a lateral motion in passing from one slot to the other. In this case the different gear sleeves have separate forks and actuating rods which are selected by the hand lever and its connections as the lever is moved sideways. Strong spring retainers should be fitted for automatically locking the rods, forks and gear sleeves that are not at the moment under the direct control of the hand lever.

A special catch of some sort should be provided to prevent the gear lever being moved so as to bring the reverse into action in mistake for one of the forward gears.

The Live Axle.

To the rear end of the first gearshaft is connected, by a universal joint, the cardan-shaft proper. The power is transmitted to the balance-geared axle by bevel or by worm gearing, and the speed reduction between the motor and road wheels is made at this point, the bevel pinion on the cardan-shaft being only a fraction of the size of the bevel wheel on the balance gear casing. Sometimes a second universal joint is introduced near the rear end of the cardan-shaft. To be really universal, the two axes of the joint should intersect, but this is seldom the case, and it is not of great importance. The joints are used to compensate for the movement of the springs, which, of course, in this case, come between the road wheels and the frame on which the variable gear box is mounted. The parts of the shaft should be as nearly as possible in line during average running conditions; otherwise, an excessive amount of work will be put on the joint or joints. Some longitudinal play should also be provided for in the shaft.

In this type of transmission the road wheels are driven direct by the parts of the balance-geared axle, which is called a "live axle" to distinguish it from the non-rotating axle on which the road wheels revolve in a chain-geared car. The parts of the live axle are mounted in bearings in a tubular casing, which is in turn secured to the rear springs, and thus to the frame of the car. The casing is enlarged centrally to inclose the balance gear and driving bevel wheel, and also to inclose and provide a bearing for the bevel pinion. In fact, a bearing ought to be, and often is, provided for the tail end of the cardan-shaft both in front of and behind the pinion, as it is very important that the relative positions of the bevel pinion and bevel wheel should be perfectly maintained. Not only is there a tendency for the bevel wheels to push apart, but, owing to the resistance to propulsion offered by the road wheels, the pinion tries to climb up the bevel wheel, and so rotate the axle casing. This should be met by providing the casing with a radial arm, which should extend forward about as far as the forward universal joint in the cardan-shaft, where it should be connected firmly, or with a small amount of elasticity, to the car frame. A neat way of resisting the rotative tendency of the live axle casing is to dispense with the rear universal joint and continue the part of the casing containing the tail of the shaft, along the shaft, nearly to the front universal joint. This answers the purpose well, and makes for simplicity at the same time.

The Gear-box.

The spur wheels of the change speed gear are inclosed in a gear-box, which serves several purposes: first, to provide a framework in which the spindles may be mounted in bearings of fixed relative position; second, to exclude dirt and wet, and, third, to hold a quantity of gear-case oil for lubricating the wheel teeth. The spindle bearings are usually lubricated with oil through pipes leading from the lubricator on the dashboard. The balance gear is similarly inclosed and lubricated.

Control of the Gear.

The principle on which most modern gears are modeled is described above, but there are many variations. The most popular consists in having two sliding sleeves instead of one. There are several advantages in this. The shafts can be made much smaller, which minimizes the tendency to spring and reduces the noise in the gears. The gear-box, too, can be made neater and lighter.

In the two sliding sleeves type of gear, of course, there is a shifting fork for each pair of sliding gears, as well as for the reverse. In order that these three forks can be operated by one lever, and so that no two sets of gears can be put into engagement at the same time, which would entail serious damage to the mechanism, what is known as the gate control is used.

The hand lever at the side of the car, which is used to operate the change speed gear, works in a quadrant having three parallel slots with a short cross slot joining them. The lever cannot only be moved forward and backward, but also can be slid sideways, carrying with it the short lever which engages with the three rods which operate the three sliding forks of the gear. Each rod has at its end a claw or slot, and as the lever is moved sideways through the slot connecting the three parallel slots in the quadrant, it engages with one or the other of the three claws. Until the lever is moved into a position where it can be pulled through from one slot to the other it cannot, of course, be disconnected from the claw and rod which it is operating, and when it is moved into such position the rod is so situated that the pair of gears it operates are not in mesh with any other wheel.

Direct Drive on Top Speed.

A variation of the gear wheel sliding type of change speed which has proved very popular is that in which the drive is direct on the top speed. In this the drive is taken from the end of the primary gearshaft to the countershaft or propeller shaft as the case may be, and is absolutely direct from the engine on the top speed. On the other speeds the drive is transmitted from the forward portion of the primary shaft to the secondary shaft, and thence back to the rear portion of the primary shaft. From this point it is transmitted in the usual way. In this arrangement the direct drive on top speed is noiseless and particularly efficient, for the drive is not transmitted through any of the gear wheels, and there is one less change of direction than in the chain-driven type. On the other speeds, however, there is one additional change of direction as compared with the chain-driven type, and an additional pair of gear wheels is in operation, causing increased friction and noise.

Some designers arrange for having the third speed direct instead of the fourth, and this variation has something to recommend it, for, with a third speed a little higher than usual it practically becomes the normal, and the high speed is only used when the drive is comparatively light, and a little extra friction is not of so much consequence. Besides, the large gear wheels of the high speed do not make as much noise as the smaller gear wheels of an indirect third would do.

A variation which has been adopted by some important firms has a good deal to recommend it and seems likely to become more popular. Its object is to combine the advantages of both the leading types; that is to say, while the drive is direct on the top speed there is only a single change of direction in the others, as in the case of the standard Panhard type. This variation is fitted to Mercedes cars.

Direct Drive on all Speeds.

There are certain cars which have a direct drive on all three speeds, and the arrangement may be described as follows: The change speed gear-box is on the back axle. The propeller shaft has mounted on its extremity three bevel pinions which mesh with three bevel wheels of different sizes on the live back axle. These bevel wheels are free to revolve on the axle unless locked to it by a sliding expanding star key. A change of speed is effected by locking each set of these wheels alternately to the axle, the other two meanwhile running free. Another bevel wheel mounted on the opposite side of the live axle from the three loose bevels similarly gives the reverse when locked to the live axle. The gear is in the out-of-drive or neutral position when none of the bevel wheels are locked to the live axle.

Gears in Mesh and Sliding Feather.

The sliding feather engagement consists of an arrangement, as the name indicates, of sliding feathers which determine which pair of wheels in the gear-box transmit the power, all the others running loose on their shafts and being constantly in mesh.

Constantly Meshing Gears Operated by Clutches.

There are several types of these operated respectively by expanding, positive, and frictional clutch arrangements. They possess two characteristics in particular of great value, namely, (1) very short shafts can be adopted, and (2) the gear wheels being in mesh the teeth cannot be injured by clumsy manipulation, and the arrangement is, consequently, to a considerable extent, fool-proof.

The Expanding Clutch System.

The De Dion gear may be taken as an example of this type. On the secondary shaft are mounted clutch boxes to which are fixed the gear wheels, both boxes and gear wheels normally revolving idly on the shaft. Inside the clutch boxes are expanding fiber-faced clutches fixed on the shaft and operated by a lever on the steering column and a ratchet inside the hollow shaft. By expanding one or other of these clutches the corresponding box with its gear wheel becomes fixed to the secondary shaft, and so communicates the drive to the bevel pinion and then by the bevel wheel to the rear axle.

The Friction Clutch System.

This is well exemplified by the change speed gear which is illustrated. The diagram gives a sectional view through

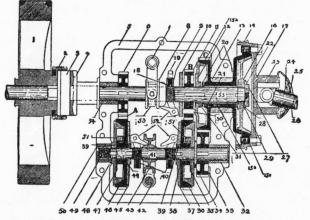

Change Speed Gear with Friction Clutch.

the center of the gear-box. It has two forward speeds and a reverse.

No. 55 is the primary shaft driven by the engine, and on this shaft are mounted the driving pinions, 6 and 11, revolving always with it; 41 is the secondary shaft on which are mounted to run freely the gear wheels 46 and 36. On the shaft 41 is also a pinion 33, which is fixed to it, and is always revolving, and meshes always with the gear wheel 15A, which is part of a sleeve 15B surrounding the right-hand end of the primary shaft 55, and running in the long bearing and free to run independently of the shaft 55. At the outer end of this sleeve 15B, is the clutch 15C, its male portion 16 engaging with it.

The two gear wheels, 46 and 36, are provided with clutches by means of which they can be gripped to the shaft. 46 is in constant mesh with a gear wheel not shown, which is in turn meshed always to the pinion 6. 36 is always in mesh with 11. It will be seen therefore that when the primary shaft is rotating, the gear wheels, 46 and 36, are also rotating, 46 in the same direction as the primary shaft, and 36 in the opposite direction. While thus rotating on the shaft 41 they run on anti-friction sleeves.

The drive from the gear is taken direct from the clutch 15c on the sleeve 15b, which is always revolving with the cardan-shaft and the rear live axle. The shaft 55 revolves constantly with the engine, being coupled by a flexible joint direct to the flywheel boss.

Two hand-levers are used to operate the gear. One for the top speed, which is direct, and the other for the low speed and the reverse, which are by means of the secondary shaft. These hand-levers simply put in and out of operation the three clutches which operate the gears.

We shall first describe the drive on the top speed, which is direct.

It will be seen that inside the gear wheel 15a on the sleeve 15b is a coned clutch male member 12 which revolves with the primary shaft 55, but is free to slide slightly along it. A similar male clutch member 16 is fixed at the end of the shaft 55, and between these two clutch members the sleeve 15b can be rigidly nipped. To bring the two clutch members together there are provided three pivoted dogs shown at 52, pivoted on a collar screwed and clamped to the shaft 55. The small ends of the dogs press against a disk 10, which in turn presses three pins, one of which is shown at 30. These pass through holes in the pinion wheel 11, and in turn press against the male clutch member 12. The long ends of the dogs come into contact with a sliding cone 8 on a collar which can slide along the shaft and is operated by the fork 7 connected with the hand lever.

When the collar 53 is slid along to the right it lifts the long ends of the dogs, the shorter ends pressing with considerable force against the disk 10, and drawing together the two male clutch members 12 and 16, gripping the sleeve 15b firmly between them and causing it to revolve with the shaft 55. This is the top speed, with a direct drive right through from the engine crank shaft to differential gear on the rear axle. During the time that the direct top speed is in operation it will be understood that the shaft 41 is revolving, and the gear wheels 46 and 36 are also revolving upon it, both at different speeds, and one in the opposite direction (46).

We shall now describe the operation of the low gear. During this operation the clutch 12-16 is, of course, free, and the sleeve 15b is free of the primary shaft. The low speed is driven by the pinion 11, which is, as we have seen, keyed to the shaft 55, and meshes with the gear wheel 36, normally running free on the shaft 41. This gear wheel 36 is provided with a clutch consisting of the male cone 34 keyed to shaft 41 on one side of it, and a flat disk 37 free to slide, but not turn, upon the shaft 41. Similar dogs to that described for the top gear clutch, and one of which is shown at 52, are used to force the disk 37 up against the back of the gear wheel 36, and in turn to force this into engagement with the male clutch member 34. When this clutch, therefore, is in operation the pinion 11 drives the gear wheel 36. This being now engaged with the shaft 41 the latter revolves with it, and the pinion 33 keyed upon it drives the sleeve 15b through the medium of the gear wheel 15a, which is part and parcel of the sleeve 15b, from which the drive is direct to the back axle. The dogs are operated by the sliding cone 43, which in this case is double-ended, the right-hand end operating the clutch we have just described, and the left-hand end operating the reverse, with which we shall now deal.

The reverse gear is driven by the pinion 6 keyed to the

shaft 55. This pinion drives a second pinion, which is not shown in our diagram, but which is, in turn, in mesh with the gear wheel 46, which it consequently keeps constantly turning in the same direction as the shaft 55, but at a lower speed. This gear wheel 46 is also provided with a clutch operated similarly to the low-speed clutch by one of the dogs shown at 52. When the ends of these dogs are forced up by the movement of the cone along the shaft they press the flat disk 45 up against the flat face of the gear wheel 46, and force it into engagement with the male cone member 48 rigidly mounted on the shaft. The shaft 41 must then turn with the wheel 46 and in the same direction and at the same speed, so that the pinion 6 drives 46 (through the intermediate pinion) in the same direction as itself; 46, being now rigid with the shaft, transmits motion in the opposite direction through the medium of the pinion 33 to the gear wheel on the sleeve 15b, and so drives the car in the reverse direction.

The arrangement of the clutches is such that there is no end thrust on the shafts on which they operate. The collars which carry the pivoted dogs 52 are screwed on to the shafts, and can be adjusted nearer or further away from the clutches by simply screwing them round. When adjusted, they are clamped to the shaft by the pinching screws 40 and 19. The clutches are kept normally out of engagement by small helical springs between the male and female portions of the clutches. Four of these springs are shown in our illustration. In this particular arrangement there is no main clutch. As will be seen, the engine can be declutched from the car by operating any of the change speed gear levers.

Epicycloidal Gears.

The epicyclic or "crypto" type of gear has come very largely into use for automobile transmission purposes. The arrangements vary largely, and form the subject matter of many patents, but, generally speaking, the gears approximate very closely to one another, and the changes of speed are obtained by rendering different elements stationary or active.

In one typical form of epicyclic gearing a center or sun wheel is surrounded by an internally-toothed wheel of considerably larger diameter. One or more planet pinions are mounted on a carrier and gear with both the other wheels. All the wheels are in one plane and form a concentric system. By locking the sun wheel, the internally-toothed wheel, or the pinion-carrier to either the driving or the driven parts, and by holding one or other of them stationary, forward and reverse motions can be obtained at different ratios. The wheels are always in mesh, and the changes of speed are brought about by the application of brake bands, and, therefore, without shock.

A number of transmission gears have been devised in which the motor-shaft and other shafts are all arranged transversely of the car and so parallel to one another. The various speeds are generally obtained by means of sliding spur wheels, and the motion is conveyed from shaft to shaft by chains.

The parallel system of transmission should, theoretically, be considerably more efficient than systems in which the power is carried round one or more right angles, but the theory is not well borne out in such severely practical tests as hill-climbing competitions. The restrictions of space make it difficult to set a large motor transversely of the car.

Belt Drive Gearing.

Other systems of change speed gearing have been in use from time to time, but are now obsolete. Of these the belt drive was at one time most popular, especially in Europe, in connection with cars of the Benz make. It had considerable advantages in the way of silence, smoothness of working and simplicity; but the constant stretching, slipping and breaking of the belts, due largely to the use of unsuitable material and exposure to wet and mud, and some lack of efficiency, gradually led to its abandonment, though it may possibly come in again for small cars.

Usually the arrangement for belt-drive comprised two pulleys of unequal diameters, securely keyed to the motor shaft and driving a countershaft, from which the power was transmitted by side chains to the wheels. The drums on the motor shaft were made double the width of those on the countershaft, so as to permit of lateral movement of the driving belt. The countershaft pulleys were in pairs, one fast and the second loose, and set alternately with the remaining pulleys driven by the other belt, so that when the countershaft was being driven from the motor shaft by, say, the high-speed drum, the low-speed belt was on its loose pulley and out of action.

The belts were shifted by forks operated from the driver's seat, and arrangements were made that the striking gear should first let both belts run loose, and then set the low gear in operation, a further movement freeing the low speed, and allowing the high gear to come into action.

When belt-driven cars were in vogue attempts were made to vary the gear by regulating the amount of slip of the belt. Experiments have since been made with a system of driving by means of a large circular disk, against which is pressed a leather-faced wheel, connected with the countershaft.

The Auto-Mixte Gear.

An idea which does not come under any of the heads already dealt with is to be found in the Auto-Mixte, a Belgian car. Instead of a change-speed gear, a dynamo and accumulators, or storage battery cells, are used, and the clutch and brake are magnetic.

Under ordinary conditions, the engine drives direct through the armature of an electric dynamo to a magnetic clutch of the disk type, and thence direct to the rear live axle. The dynamo is shunt wound, and when the load of the engine is light, part of its power is utilized to generate current in the field of the dynamo, which current is stored in an accumulator consisting of 28 cells connected in series. When the load on the engine is heavy the dynamo may be used as a motor to assist it, the current being supplied from the accumulators. By means of a controller the speed can be varied by sometimes letting the engine drive the rear axle only—letting it partly drive the rear axle and partly charge the accumulator, or by letting it drive the rear axle, assisted by the motor. The controller is operated by a hand lever at the side of the driver and suitable, ampere and volt meters are arranged to show exactly the condition electrically of the accumulator and the dynamo.

A specialty in this system is the magnetic clutch. The end of the motor shaft carries a large electro-magnet facing a flat disk mounted on the propeller shaft. A similar electro-magnet is held stationary in the car frame, and faces the back of the disk. When current is passed through the coils of the motor shaft magnets, they magnetically clutch the disk and transmit the drive. When current is passed through the coils of the stationary magnets they similarly attract the disk and act as a powerful brake. A hand controller, determining the voltage of the current passing through the magnet, allows of the engagement or disengagement of the clutch being accomplished gradually.

The Art of Gear Changing.

To effect the change appropriate to the grade swiftly and without noise, without loss of way and without shock to the car, or accidental disturbance of the steering, and without racing the engine, is generally supposed to constitute the whole art of gear changing. It is an important part, but only a part, for there still remains the question of making the change at exactly the right time.

When the car on its top gear comes to a uniformly graded hill, steep enough to cause the speed to fall off in spite of the throttle having been fully opened and the spark adjusted to its best position, which must be known, the driver can at his will and discretion allow the engine to continue to pull for a considerable time on that gear, but with the engine getting gradually slower and consequently developing less and less horse-power. To a certain extent this is what he should do to get the best result from his car, provided that he changes down to a lower gear at that moment precisely when he can just maintain his speed with the speed lever in the new position. As a test of changing at the right time, it is to be noted that if the hill continues to be of uniform slope, a good driver when seeking for the best possible speed of traveling should not find that the car gains speed on the lower gear, for that would prove that he changed too late—unless perchance he was driving with the specific object of economizing in gasolene.

A bad driver is as likely to change too early as too late, that is to say he will change gear at a moment when the engine cannot rotate fast enough with the lower gear ratio to attain to the speed which he already had. He then not only loses speed and wastes time, but he wastes gasolene and does no good to his engine by racing it.

A little practice shows the driver that an appreciable amount of way is lost during the brief interval between the unclutching and reclutching necessary for the change of gear, so that when he is near the summit of a. hill he often deems it policy from the point of view of time and fuel saved, to avoid interrupting even for so brief a time the action of the engine. He remembers that as soon as the crest of the hill has been surmounted, there will be a second waste of time in changing up again to the top notch.

What Happens in the Gear-Box.

The ordinary gear requires that the teeth of the wheels which are in mesh shall be disengaged, and others substituted in their place by a sliding movement.

Suppose the car in motion with any one set of gear wheels, when it becomes expedient to change gear. The person driving, first, and before pulling the speed lever, presses down a pedal so as to disengage his clutch. The effect of this is that the engine no longer transmits any power to the road wheels through the gear, though the gear still rotates by its own inertia. Then with the speed lever he disengages one pair of wheels and quickly attempts to thread the teeth of the pinion he wants to use into the spaces of another pinion which stands ready on the shaft which drives the road wheels.

If the spaces are just opposite the teeth and rotating at the same pace they will slip into place sweetly; if not, there is grinding and perhaps a few bruised teeth. Practice alone can teach the exact amount of hurry to use in pushing the new pinion into place, but in no case should any strong muscular effort be expended on the lever. In gear changing the driver must work accurately, gently and at the right moment.

Selective Sliding Gear.

In the most modern American parlance the type of change speed gear or transmission in which any change can be made without passing through the intermediate gears is known as selective system. Thus, in the 1909 Winton six-cylinder car, for example, the gear change mechanism is of this type, supported on annular ball bearings, with three forward speeds and reverse. There is direct drive on the third speed through internal and external gear combination. The selective mechanism makes it possible to enter neutral position, but impossible to engage any new set of gears while the clutch is engaged.

PART XVI.

DON'TS FOR MOTOR-CAR DRIVERS.

Don'ts—The following "Don'ts" should be heeded by all owners and operators of gasolene engines:

Don't tear your engine to pieces if it will not run. The trouble will, in all probability, be located by one of the following tests:

Turn your engine over and see if the compression is correct.

See if you have a spark.

See that the gasolene supply is correct and has no water in it.

See that the needle valve of carbureter is not clogged with dirt.

See that the engine valves are not stuck and that they seat quickly. They should be reground once every year.

1. Don't fail to read instructions on Starting the Engine.

2. Don't forget to keep cylinder lubricator filled and feeding. A dry piston will greatly reduce the power and cut the cylinder or piston.

3. Don't think that the cylinder should be perfectly cold. A gasolene engine works best when it is warm.

4. Don't keep the cylinder too hot or too cold. See that the air has full circulation. It is as necessary as gasolene. An engine can not pull a load if overheated.

5. Don't forget to throw switch out when engine is not in use.

6. Don't forget to shut off gasolene when not running.

7. Don't try to make any improvements on your engine without notifying the makers first.

8. Don't fail to use the kind of cylinder oil recommended

by the maker. It may be better than the more expensive grades.

9. Don't try to wipe engine while in motion.

10. Don't use too much gasolene. The engine develops the most power when working on a smokeless mixture. A black smoke coming from exhaust means too much gasolene; a blue smoke means too much lubricating oil.

11. Don't try to start engine with cylinder full of gasolene. Shut off same and turn engine over a few times before trying again.

12. Don't fail to see that everything is ready before trying to start engine.

13. Don't forget that nine times out of ten when the engine will not run you are at fault. Look around you and see what you have forgotten. It does no good to turn over the engine if conditions are not right.

14. Don't fail to look your engine over carefully when it is in first-class condition. You will then know how to fix it when something goes wrong.

15. Don't fail to have a fine gauze screen put in your funnel and strain all gasolene put in the tank.

16. Don't allow the working parts of engine to knock or hammer. Pay special attention to the connecting rod and keep it as tight as will allow engine to turn easily and run cool.

17. Don't think your engine will not wear out and that it does not need some care.

18. Don't be afraid to try and fix your own engine. You can not tell what a good job you can do until you have tried.

19. Don't allow dirt or dust to accumulate on top of your batteries, as there is danger of short-circuiting them.

20. Don't forget to see that the wires are tight on the batteries and that they may become exhausted in five or six months.

21. Don't run electric bells with engine battery and don't let your engine stand outdoors without some cover for protection from rain. If the batteries become wet they will be short circuited and become useless.

22. Don't forget to look into the gasolene tank before sending for an expert. This seems simple but it has been omitted many times at great expense.

23. Don't forget "Don't" number seven.

The engine will never stop from other than one of the following causes:

24. Gasolene supply exhausted.

25. Air circulation not sufficient.

26. Overload.

27. Gasolene pipe obstructed or the connections loose.

28. Battery failing or broken wire.

29. Spark being set out of time or a short circuit in the insulation of the spring.

30. Not enough oil, or poor oil on piston.

31. Bearings not lubricated and sticking.

32. Intake or exhaust stem sticking or leaking valves.

33. Packing blowing out.

34. Exhaust spring becoming weak or some part becoming disconnected or broken.

35. The gasolene pipe being clogged or having a loose joint.

36. The spark plug becoming short-circuited.

37. Parts can only become disconnected by neglect to keep them tightened properly.

38. Breakages can only occur by some obstruction coming in contact with moving parts, some objects striking engine; or, some part getting loose or disconnected.

39. The screw of the spark coil sticking to the spring. Smooth off the points.

The engine will not run unsteadily from other than the following causes:

40. Lack of oil on all governor bearings, especially collar.

41. Governor out of adjustment by someone changing it, or natural wear.

42. By the catch plate on the end of governor lever becoming worn, so it will not hold up the push lever during the idle strokes of the engine.

43. By the governor lever becoming out of adjustment so

its catch plate can't engage the projection on the push lever when it has been pushed out by the cam.

44. Gasolene valve not properly regulated.

45. Obstruction of gasolene pipe by water or otherwise.

46. If using battery, the battery becoming weak and missing fire.

47. The spark plug points fouled with oil, soot or rust. The exhaust spring becoming weak.

48. The exhaust or intake valve stem sticking slightly, but not enough to stop engine.

49. The accumulation of dirt and grit in any of the governor bearings.

50. The insulation of the insulated spark plug spring becoming short circuited.

51. The exhaust or intake valve leaking.

A Few "Knox" Don'ts.

Below are a few Don'ts urged by the manufacturers upon the attention of all purchasers of "Knox" cars.

Don't start the motor until certain that the spark and throttle control levers are in their proper position (spark lever at highest point on sector; throttle advanced one-quarter way; gear shift lever in neutral position on inside of speed gears).

Don't let the clutch drop in; let in gradually.

Don't start car on other than first speed.

Don't start car with brakes applied.

Don't let engine race or run at a high speed when car is standing idle.

Don't let car stand with gear shift in other than neutral position.

Don't let car stand on hill without applying emergency brake.

Don't advance throttle too far when starting car.

Don't try to run without oil, water or gasolene.

Don't drive fast around corners; it is dangerous and destructive to tires.

"Don'ts" for Drivers.

The following "Don'ts" by Mr. Dave H. Morris, former president of the Automobile Club of America and member of the Committee on Public Safety are also well worth heeding:

1. Don't disobey the rules of the road.—Remember to keep to the right and pass on the left.

2. Don't forget that pedestrians have the same rights as vehicles at street crossings.—Remember that vehicles do not have the right of way at street crossings.

3. Don't forget that your rate of speed should never exceed the legal rate, whatever it may be.—Remember, when local conditions require, to adopt even a lower rate of speed than the legal rate.

4. Don't get "rattled."—Remember that it is the "other fellow" who always loses his head in a crisis.

5. Don't insist upon your rights.—Remember that the "other fellow" may not know your rights, and an insistance on your part is bound to result in an accident.

6. Don't argue with trolley-cars, express-wagons, brewery-trucks, or other heavy bodies found in the public thoroughfare.—Remember that the drivers of these powerful vehicles generally operate on the theory that might is right.

7. Don't expect women and children to get out of your way.—Remember that many women and children don't know how to avoid danger.

8. Don't run any unnecessary risks.—Remember that while the automobile is flexible, powerful, and easily operated, you may make a slip.

9. Don't drink.—Remember that nine-tenths of the accidents occur to automobiles driven by intoxicated chauffeurs.

10. Don't sneak away in case of an accident.—Remember that the true gentleman chauffeur, although he may not be responsible for the misfortune, stands his ground.

11. Don't fail to be a gentleman under any provocation.—Remember that the Golden Rule practised on the road will save you no end of trouble, expense, and worry.

DON'TS FOR TIRE OWNERS.

Do not apply brakes so hard as to skid the wheels; this is what tears tires to pieces.

Do not round corners at top speed; remember that in turning corners, particularly when a car is loaded, there is great strain on the tires. Figure this out.

Do not let the tires rub the curb; the steering knuckle may become bent and the tires badly worn on one side.

Do not let in the clutch so that the car starts with a jerk; this tears the tread of the tires and is apt to part the rubber from the fabric.

Do not permit water to creep between the tires and the rims; the fabric will be rotted from the water and from the rust that will form on the rims.

Do not run at speed over roads that have rocks or crushed stone on the surface; give the tires a chance to respond to the inequalities of the road.

Do not drive in street car tracks; they will cut the tires on the outside edge in a short time.

Do not take railroad tracks, bridges, crosswalks, etc., head on and at speed; take them at an angle and slow down, so as to avoid pinching the inner tube.

Do not **guess** the tires have enough air; put on a gauge and **know** it.

Do not go out without an extra casing, two extra tubes, a repair kit, a pump and an air bottle. The last-named is one of the blessings of motoring; it has taken away half the troubles.

Do not become hasty or excited in making a tire repair; time will always be saved by taking things as they come and making the best of them.

Do not permit a car to rest on a deflated tire; it will soon cut the casing and pinch the tube.

Do not fail to use talcum or soapstone in the casing when making a change or when putting in a new tube; it prevents friction and adhesion.

Do not let lug nuts, valve nuts, valve caps, rim nuts, or any other part become loose.

Do not let the valve stem be exposed to mud and dirt; secure a cap for it and always use it.

Do not run a tire flat; if necessary, because of the absence of another casing or repair kit, remove the casing and destroy the rim rather than the casing—it will be cheaper. Better still, procure some rope and make a temporary tire, first removing the casing.

Do not permit small holes or cuts to go unvulcanized; a stitch in time is a certainty in this case.

Do not throw the extra inner tube under the seat and amid all the other stuff carried; deflate it, wrap it in a water-proof bag and pack it away carefully.

Do not forget a few extra valves to be carried in the repair kit.

Do not use tire chains more than is absolutely necessary; they can do the tires no good.

Do not drive on the side of the road when it can be avoided; this puts a terrific strain on the tires.

Do not stint yourself on the use of free air.

Do not permit wheels out of true to remain so; they will soon wear out the tires. Wheels should track; axles should be straight.

Do not permit grease or oil to remain on tires; clean with gasolene and dry immediately.

Do not permit rims to become rusty; cover with enamel, paint or shellac. Before applying tires, coat the rim with graphite and the tire will be easy to remove.